Crazy Like a Fox

Crazy Like a Fox

The Inside Story of How Fox News Beat CNN

Scott Collins

Portfolio

PORTFOLIO
Published by the Penguin Group
Penguin Group (USA) Inc., 375 Hudson Street,
New York, New York 10014, U.S.A.
Penguin Books Ltd, 80 Strand,
London WC2R 0RL, England
Penguin Books Australia Ltd, 250 Camberwell Road, Camberwell,
Victoria 3124, Australia
Penguin Books Canada Ltd, 10 Alcorn Avenue,
Toronto, Ontario, Canada M4V 3B2
Penguin Books India (P) Ltd, 11 Community Centre, Panchsheel Park,
New Delhi–110 017, India
Penguin Books (N.Z.) Ltd, Cnr Rosedale and Airborne Roads, Albany,
Auckland, New Zealand
Penguin Books (South Africa) (Pty) Ltd, 24 Sturdee Avenue,
Rosebank, Johannesburg 2196, South Africa

Penguin Books Ltd, Registered Offices:
80 Strand, London WC2R 0RL, England

First published in 2004 by Portfolio,
a member of Penguin Group (USA) Inc.

1 3 5 7 9 10 8 6 4 2

LIBRARY OF CONGRESS CATALOGING-IN-PUBLICATION DATA

Collins, Scott.
Crazy like a fox : the inside story of how Fox News beat CNN / Scott Collins.
p. cm.
Includes index.
ISBN 1-59184-029-5
1. Television broadcasting of news—United States—History.
2. Fox News. 3. Cable News Network. I. Title.

PN4888.T4C65 2004
070.4'3'0973—dc22 2003068955

This book is printed on acid-free paper.

Printed in the United States of America
Set in Bembo
Designed by Erin Benach

To Harry Raney
and to Elena and Gabby

Acknowledgments

This book would not have been possible without the generous and sometimes courageous cooperation of many people at CNN, Fox News, and MSNBC.

At Fox News, I owe a special debt to Brian Lewis, who opened countless doors and provided critical information every step of the way, assisted by his staffers Irena Briganti, Paul Schur, and Robert Zimmerman. I'm also enormously grateful to Roger Ailes, whose life story is worth a book or two in itself and who was, as ever, an eloquent and witty raconteur. And there's no way I can repay Chet Collier, Brit Hume, John Moody, Bill O'Reilly, Bill Shine, Shepard Smith, and Greta Van Susteren for the recollections they provided, not to mention the kindnesses they bestowed, over the months I was researching the book.

At News Corp., I'm grateful for guidance from Andrew Butcher, Terry Everett, Chase Carey, and Nicky Weinstock. Scott Grogin of Fox Broadcasting Company was also most helpful.

At CNN, I am thankful for patient assistance from Christa Robinson and Matt Furman, as well as from Shirley Powell of Turner Broadcasting. The remembrances of three former CNN bosses—Walter Isaacson, Tom Johnson, and Reese Schonfeld—were all the more valuable for their candor about their tenures at the network. And a number of past and present CNN and Turner executives and on-air personalities offered invaluable insight and help, including Garth Ancier, Aaron Brown, Greg D'Alba, Lou Dobbs, Steve Haworth, Bill Hemmer, Eason Jordan, Rick Kaplan, Jamie Kellner, Jim Miller, Teya Ryan, Brad Turell, Robert Wussler, and Paula Zahn.

At MSNBC, I was fortunate to receive help from Erik Sorenson, the network's president and general manager, not to mention Paulette Song and Jeremy Gaines. Phil Griffin, Peter Neupert, Mark O'Connor, and Brian Williams were also valuable sources, especially about the early history of the network.

NBC's Bob Wright spoke candidly about the creation and performance of MSNBC, as did his former lieutenants, Andy Lack and Tom Rogers. Kassie Canter, formerly of NBC, as well as NBC's Cory Shields and Alex Constantinople of General Electric, were also tremendously kind, patient, and helpful sources.

Several other people provided valuable insights about the television news business generally, among them Jeff Gralnick, Steve Friedman, Richard Leibner, Jonathan Wald, and Richard Wald. As he has been to so many people in Hollywood, Alan Berger was a trusted friend and wise counsel throughout the process of reporting and writing this book.

A few sources spoke on the condition that they not be identified. They know who they are, and each earned my sincere gratitude.

Thankful as I am for the help from these knowledgeable sources, it should be pointed out that none of the networks or companies involved in any way authorized this book, and whatever conclusions (and, alas, errors or oversights) it contains are my own.

My friend and former coworker Jennifer Morton deserves special thanks for research beyond the call of duty.

Howard Burns, Bob Dowling, and Cynthia Littleton, my editors at *The Hollywood Reporter,* generously granted me a leave to work on the project, as well as two lengthy extensions. I am deeply appreciative.

Many colleagues offered help, encouragement, and guidance along the way, among them Kurt Andersen, Steve Brill, Steve Battaglio, Michael Cieply, Lisa DeMoraes, John Higgins, Michael Hirschorn, Ted Johnson, Brian Lowry, Dennis McDougal, Mary Murphy, Kyle Pope, Max Robins, Jim Rutenberg, and Ed Wasserman.

Writing a book is such a solitary and grueling endeavor that good friends become even more treasured than usual. Bill Concannon, Peter

Giaquinta, Bill Hawkins, Patrick McGavin, Adrian Maher, and Reece Pendleton are the world's best.

Anyone who knows Eric Simonoff knows he's one hell of a great agent. Eric believed in this project from its earliest stages and made the dream a reality. I am forever in his debt. Big thanks, too, to Brian Lipson, who saw to it that the project fell into Eric's hands.

All writers should be so lucky as to be read by Stephanie Land, my judicious editor at Portfolio. A more sympathetic sounding board you could not find, but she also kicked my butt (in a good way) exactly when I needed it. And to Portfolio's Adrian Zackheim, deep thanks for not only buying this book, but also "getting it" from the very start. You are the man.

My sister, Terese Paulson, and brother, Mark Collins, and my parents, Esther and Ed Collins, were enthusiastic cheerleaders. Tom Preston listened to an awful lot of gripes and excuses over the past seven years, all the while encouraging me to keep my eyes on the prize.

My wife, Elena, and our daugther, Gabby, have been a never-ending source of joy, love, and support for me. If I have any regret related to this project, it's the months I spent neglecting the two most important people in the world to me.

And thanks most of all to Harry Raney, who practically ordered me to write for a living more than twenty years ago at Ridgeway High School in Memphis, Tennessee. Of course I had little idea at the time that there are far easier ways of making one's way in the world. But I pray now, as I did then, that his faith in me was warranted.

Contents

Crazy Like a Fox

Prologue

"I hate the news. News is evil. It makes people feel bad." —Ted Turner, several years before founding CNN, in Porter Bibb, *Ted Turner*

Gulf War II was barely twenty-four hours old when CNN lost its first major battle.

"You're worse than the American administration," an Iraqi censor fumed to Nic Robertson after summoning the CNN correspondent from his room at Baghdad's Palestine Hotel on the afternoon of March 21, 2003. "Get out of Iraq! Get out immediately!"

Early the next morning, Robertson and his crew reluctantly piled into their vehicle for the four-hundred-mile trip west through the desert to the Jordanian border. The forty-year-old Robertson, who reported from Iraq during Operation Desert Storm eleven years earlier, had expected to be the only staff reporter for an American network remaining in Baghdad, filing dramatic live dispatches as U.S. and British troops besieged the city. Instead, he was catching his last fleeting glimpses of life in the bomb-wracked Iraqi capital, as heavily armed members of Saddam Hussein's Baath Party darted past shattered storefronts and slipped inside bunkers.

Robertson's forced exit was a grimly ironic setback for CNN, which earmarked an extra $35 million just to cover Gulf War II. Network executives were hoping for a dramatic replay of the first Persian Gulf War, when CNN had become a global icon for its journalistic fortitude in Baghdad. During the early morning of January 16, 1991, CNN correspondents Peter Arnett, John Holliman, and Bernard Shaw huddled into Suite 906 of the Al-Rashid Hotel. Among the last American reporters in the city, the trio reported live by four-wire telephone as U.S. forces ravaged Baghdad in one of the most ferocious air raids in military history. The worldwide audience was estimated at 1 billion—the largest in history for a nonsporting event. Just as narrative music videos from Michael Jackson and Madonna had validated the newborn MTV in the early 1980s, now the Gulf War had propelled CNN into the international spotlight. Broadcast news veterans bolted upright as the air sounded with a strange new battle cry: "Turn on CNN."

The Desert Storm triumph was delicious revenge for the eccentric Atlanta mogul Ted Turner, who founded CNN in 1980. The twenty-four-hour Cable News Network was initially so unpolished, and staffed with so many low-paid neophytes, that rivals derided the enterprise as "Chicken Noodle News." When critics predicted that Turner's new cable service would quickly end in defeat, he vowed that the little startup would cover the end of the world "and sign off playing 'Nearer My God to Thee.'" After the live reporting coup from CNN's "Boys of Baghdad," competitors were singing from the Turner hymnal. Despite some hair-raising early losses, Turner had proven that nonstop news coverage could make for a profitable business. "News is the star," Turner had said, and he made good on his word. Gross ad revenue at CNN exploded to $322 million in 1995, nearly double 1990's figure. By 1996, CNN was available in 68 million homes, 15 percent more than at the outbreak of Gulf War I. Ratings surged during breaking news events such as the O.J. Simpson murder trial and the Oklahoma City bombing. Cable operators reported that CNN increased interest in cable TV generally. Perhaps most important, the same broadcasters that had once scorned CNN now wanted an all-news network of their own. "Before the Gulf War, [CNN] was this unknown little cable network that nobody was watching," longtime anchor Bobbie Battista said, "and after the Gulf War, suddenly everyone is watching."

But much had changed between the two Gulf Wars, in American society as well as the media business. The partisan hurricane over the impeachment of President Clinton, and the subsequent battle over presidential election results in 2000, had deepened the anger of conservative viewers who had long believed that the mainstream media nurtured an unacknowledged liberal bias. At least in 2000, the nation was almost exactly split between Democrats and Republicans, and political attacks and counterattacks became a regular feature of the cultural landscape.

Meanwhile, the growth of cable networks was eroding the market shares of the major broadcasters. ABC, CBS, and NBC were watching the audiences for their once-authoritative evening newscasts slowly disappear; viewers were scattering elsewhere in search of news, just as they were for entertainment. At the same time, the consolidation of the media business eventually made it impossible for CNN's corporate parent, Turner Broadcating, to survive as an independent entity. Once Turner merged with a larger media company, rivals began plotting their own competing cable news services.

By the time American tanks again rolled into battle in the Persian Gulf in March of 2003, CNN found itself locked in a bitter war of its own. The network that for most of its existence held a virtual monopoly on cable news faced two competitors, MSNBC and Fox News Channel. While MSNBC appeared at first the bigger threat, it was Fox News—launched in 1996 by Australian-born media mogul Rupert Murdoch—that was pursuing the hearts of American viewers who felt abandoned by the mainstream media. Murdoch had called CNN "too liberal." Fox News would be, in the words of its memorable slogan, "Fair and Balanced." While staffers initially denied that Fox News tipped to the right, it was soon apparent that the network offered a safe haven for conservatives, with such right-leaning hosts and anchors as Bill O'Reilly, Sean Hannity, and Brit Hume.

The resulting cable news wars reveal much about the way national politics and mass media intersect in the opening years of the 21st century. Where television news once only presumed to *cover* political warfare, it now feeds it. Fox News' Bill O'Reilly—a formerly obscure tabloid TV host who has become one of the most popular news hosts on television—has used his nightly bully pulpit to stump against the Clintons, antiwar protesters, and alleged government waste. MSNBC has hired O'Reilly copycats such as Joe Scarborough, a former U.S. representative, and right-wing firebrand Michael Savage. The news networks have become part and parcel of the entertainment empires that own them, increasingly dragging the network news divisions along in a battle for ratings and interview "gets" with celebrities and newsmakers.

The story of the cable news wars involves seized opportunities and failed strategies, corporate arrogance and executive intrigue, intense battles for ratings, advertising, and multimillion dollar anchors. And the surprising outcome of this unlikely battle has changed the way Americans get—and use—the news.

1

"One Giant Leap"

"The people who get in trouble in our company are those who carry around the anchor of the past." —General Electric chairman Jack Welch, in Ken Auletta, *Three Blind Mice*

At ten o'clock on the morning of December 14, 1995, Bob Wright strode to the podium in Studio 8H at 30 Rockefeller Center, ready to unload the big secret his network had been harboring for months.

"Surprise!" the president of NBC joked as laughter rippled among the hundreds of executives and reporters gathered in the studio.

Turning serious, he added, "This is a very unprecedented announcement."

The studio was not Wright's customary habitat. Television viewers know 8H as the longtime home of *Saturday Night Live,* the place where performers such as John Belushi and Eddie Murphy made their names with comedy skits. But Wright, more than most other network executives, tended to keep his distance from showbiz glitz. He was slowly forming relationships with a few Hollywood stars—most notably Jerry Seinfeld, lead of one of NBC's most popular comedies—but Wright was hardly a natural-born showman. A former lawyer, intellectually sophisticated and somewhat prim, he concerned himself mainly with potential deals and large strategic and operational matters; specific decisions about NBC shows were usually left to his programming executives on either coast. Wright traveled so much that some staffers called him "the bumblebee," and when not flitting about on behalf of the network, he toiled from an office on the fifty-second floor of 30 Rock.

Yet on this cold, foggy Thursday, he and the other NBC brass were putting on a glitzy show of their own, unveiling a deal they hoped would change the TV news business forever. Thousands of NBC employees worldwide were watching the entire event on a live video feed, eager for details of a transaction that had only been rumored in corridors and the press. The mission was so secret that NBC executives gave it a Pentagon-like code name: The Ohio Project.

Anyone who doubted that Wright had something important to say had only to glance at the Fortune 500 celebrity who sat beside him onstage. The presence of Jack Welch highlighted any occasion. The hard-charging chairman of General Electric supervised a $60 billion conglomerate whose tentacles spread to everything from jet engines to kitchen ranges to, yes, NBC. If ranked independently, thirteen of GE's businesses would appear on the Fortune 500.

Welch had served as Wright's mentor for more than twenty years, back to the day when the rising GE exec plucked the twenty-seven-year-old lawyer from obscurity and, over internal objections, installed him as a top strategist in the plastics division. Through working together in GE's plastics, housewares, and capital divisions, Wright and his boss developed an extraordinarily close, if complicated, relationship. They bore an uncanny resemblance to each other: Both were energetic, flinty men with somewhat high-pitched voices and pale, domed foreheads surrounded by wispy fringes of graying hair. Of course there were key differences. Welch was the very definition of an alpha male, inherently restless and addicted to *change,* one of his favorite words; when he spoke publicly, he would jab his finger in the air or pound the podium for effect. Wright, by comparison, was more reflective and conservative; he tended to avoid eye contact, and when speaking publicly, his gaze was married to the TelePrompTer. Overall, though, it would be hard to find a better example of the dictum that corporate chiefs tend to promote people like themselves.

Their private lives, moreover, increasingly dovetailed with their careers. Wright owned a home across the street from Welch's in the tony Connecticut suburb of Southport, where his socially ambitious wife, Suzanne—a fixture at network parties and the self-proclaimed "First Lady of NBC"—was friendly with the former Jane Beasley, a sophisticated and intelligent mergers and acquisitions lawyer who became the GE chairman's second wife. Both men also owned vacation homes in close proximity on Nantucket.

After GE purchased RCA in 1985, pundits laughed when Welch tapped Wright to head up the NBC unit. "People wondered how a 'lightbulb maker' could run a network," Welch remembered. David Letterman, at the time host of NBC's *Late Night,* had on-air fun with running gags about Wright and GE's stewardship of the network (during the 1992–93 season, legend has it, a kite in Letterman's opening sequence bore a Japanese inscription that translated as "GE Sucks"). But no one was poking fun anymore. Under Wright's guidance, NBC was making fat profits, fueled by such hits as *Friends* and *Frasier.*

Although he had been somewhat eclipsed by the hard-charging Welch, Wright was widely regarded for his business acumen. "He has an unbelievable ability to process information," says one former NBC executive. "He really understands every aspect of NBC."

Also onstage was Andy Lack, the voluble executive credited for transforming NBC News from disarray into the number one network news division. Lack seemed forever in jeopardy of upstaging his button-down boss. On this morning, for example, with Wright clad in a dour charcoal suit with an unremarkable green necktie, Lack wore an eye-catching gray double-breasted suit with a striped shirt, brightly patterned tie, and matching maroon handkerchief blooming from the breast pocket.

Lack moved to the podium to introduce his biggest star, Tom Brokaw, live via satellite at Ramstein Air Force Base in Germany. The anchor of the *NBC Nightly News* was on assignment, reporting on U.S. troops headed for Tuzla, Bosnia. At Lack's cue, Brokaw's familiar face popped up on a giant video monitor behind Welch and Wright. The anchor was bundled in an enormous blue parka as heavy snow fell behind him on the Ramstein tarmac. Mechanics were darting about C-130 transport planes in the background.

Brokaw told the attendees how pleased he was that NBC was making this announcement and how much it would change the news business in the coming years. Then he wryly added: "Some things will not change, of course. When a big story breaks in a hostile place like this, the working stiffs will still be out in the elements, and the executives will still be in the temperature-controlled studios."

Back in New York, Lack chuckled along with the crowd, then asked Brokaw: "You wanna compare pay stubs?"

And there was yet another boldface name, the true man of the moment. On a second giant video screen, this one stage left, loomed the bespectacled image of Microsoft cofounder Bill Gates, beamed in via satellite from Hong Kong. As virtually everyone in America now knew, Gates had turned a tiny Seattle software company into a giant high-tech monopoly, along the way becoming the world's richest man. The Internet age was here, and Bill Gates was positioned to be its king.

Gates's presence confirmed, as nothing else could, that the crowd was about to witness an unveiling destined to rock the media world. It was a daring if risky move. After months of clandestine work, the secret could be told: NBC was joining forces with Microsoft to form a new twenty-four-hour cable news network that would directly target CNN.

Like other broadcast networks, NBC for years grappled with the future of its respected but costly news division. News was an important part of the broadcast mix: It attracted affluent, educated viewers, produced magazines and interview shows that could be scheduled nearly any time of day, and conferred a prestige that entertainment programs too often lacked. But news gathering was expensive. NBC, like other broadcasters, had been forced to shut down bureaus and trim news staffs in recent years.

Worse, CNN—Ted Turner's once-ridiculed cable network—had dominated perhaps the biggest news story since Watergate, the Gulf War of 1991, riding that glory to distribution and advertising gains. The Internet was likewise beginning to take hold, with its ability to update headlines at the tap of a key. NBC had to do something big soon, or the network would find itself edged out in the increasingly competitive race to provide news and information to American viewers.

Microsoft would spend $220 million to buy 50 percent of America's Talking, NBC's low-rated news and talk cable channel. Over the next six months America's Talking would transition to the new network, renamed MSNBC. In addition, Microsoft and NBC each committed at least $200 million to fund the development of a news Web site that would accompany the cable channel. One of the world's largest conglomerates was thus allied with the biggest software firm in the world, creating a Web/TV colossus that would deliver news whenever and however consumers wanted it.

Wright peered through his glasses at the reporters and executives gathered in 8H. "Today," he told the crowd, "NBC and Microsoft have come together to create news for the next millennium. . . . Both the cable and online services will be fully integrated with the NBC television network into an interlocking chain of news and information delivery that meets all levels of viewers' needs.

"No network, broadcast or cable, has ever offered news coverage of this depth, breadth, or interactivity before."

Welch summarized the parent company's view. He told listeners that he had just been invited to a centennial celebration of the Dow Jones Industrial Average and that GE was the last remaining corporation from the original index. "This company and its people have been able to adapt to change for over a hundred years," Welch said in the thick accent of his native Boston. He referred to GE as "a company that welcomes and thirsts for change." Thus it made sense, he said, for the top company of the past century to join the most dynamic and successful company of the previous decade: Microsoft.

"This is a big deal for GE," he said, "because commerce is never going to be the same again in the next decade. Commerce in the next decade will change more than it's changed in the last one hundred years. Business will be done differently, distribution will be done differently, people will buy products differently." He called Bill Gates "the most exciting entrepreneur this century may have seen."

Like a baker icing a cake, Lack slathered some of his characteristic bombast on the event. "I feel a little bit like Neil Armstrong must have felt landing on the moon," he told the crowd in 8H. "This is one small step for me and my colleagues; this is one giant leap for electronic journalism into the next century."

Sitting next to Lack onstage was Peter Neupert, who listened dazedly as the NBC executives launched into their spiel. As Microsoft's chief negotiator on the cable partnership, Neupert had spent the entire night squirreled away in Rock Center, hammering out deal points with NBC executives. He did not get one wink of sleep. Neupert was one of a half-dozen or so people in the room who knew that the "giant leap" had almost belly-flopped. Less than two hours before the news conference began, the entire deal was up for grabs.

Gates felt comfortable that Microsoft could make the online side of MSNBC profitable, but he worried that his company was going to get stuck with huge losses on the cable side. Microsoft and GE were signing a ninety-nine-year partnership agreement that would split costs and profits fifty-fifty. NBC would control the editorial functions of MSNBC, while Microsoft would control the online site. In addition to the $220 million stake in MSNBC, the software company agreed to pay a $20 million annual license fee to NBC. In return, Microsoft would get the interactive rights to all the content of NBC News—everything from MSNBC news magazines to Brokaw's *Nightly News.* But Gates wondered what would happen if NBC failed to get the new cable network into enough homes to make the whole enterprise work. Would Microsoft, a cable TV neophyte, end up eating the red ink?

Gates had good reason to be concerned. NBC executives had already started several cable channels, including CNBC and America's Talking. Microsoft, on the other hand, had virtually no experience in television programming. To strengthen its team, Microsoft had hired Ken Ziffren, a top Hollywood business attorney, to help stitch together the MSNBC deal. But Ziffren was perhaps best known for negotiating contracts on behalf of the Hollywood unions. The NBC executives soon realized that Microsoft had no one who could match their expertise in devising a complicated partnership deal for a cable TV network.

Neupert, his colleague Greg Maffei, and a Microsoft lawyer worked on the deal papers all night, trying to figure out ways to limit their company's exposure to cable losses. They continued to toil away even after Tom Rogers, the NBC Cable head, and the other GE executives filed out of the conference room around 1 A.M. But word came back that Gates, who was on a business trip to Asia, was growing increasingly anxious as time wore on. NBC had already announced the news conference, and in a few hours Rock Center would be crammed with reporters expecting to hear details of some exciting new deal. If Microsoft backed down now, "we were going to have egg on our face for a while," Neupert says.

The unflappable Neupert, a Dartmouth MBA, kept working as dawn approached. In two days he was headed with his family on a three-week vacation to Australia and New Zealand, and he wanted to hurry up and finish the MSNBC deal and get ready for the trip. He shaved in a Rock Center bathroom and slipped into a new shirt and tie he had brought along in his bags. At 7 A.M., with the lawyers haggling over contract terms governing financial liability, Rogers returned and said that Jack Welch would like to have a word with him.

Neupert had never met Welch before. To any MBA, getting an invitation from the GE chief was akin to receiving an audience with God (at one point CNBC, NBC's cable channel devoted to business news, punctuated any mention of Welch's name with strains from Handel's "Hallelujah Chorus"). "Neutron Jack" was beloved on Wall Street for his ruthless devotion to the bottom line. GE's revenues had increased threefold under his stewardship, from $27.9 billion in 1984 to $90.8 billion in 1997. The company's stock price had outperformed the overall market by at least 40 percent, according to one estimate. Once attacked for mercilessly firing tens of thousands of GE workers, Welch's unique combination of relentless cost-cutting and acquisitive fervor was now celebrated on the covers of *Fortune, Business Week,* and other magazines. And the indefatigable Welch, who had undergone open-heart surgery after a major heart attack just six months earlier, would soon unveil his crowning glory, GE's "Six Sigma" quality program aimed at reducing production errors to infinitesimal levels. Six Sigma would add to the Welch legacy a bona fide business theory, something that would help elevate his tenure to a management cult.

As it happened, early in the morning when he heard that Gates was wavering, Wright had called Welch and asked him to intervene personally. For Welch this fell under the heading of a "deep dive." Even though he ran a multinational conglomerate, the GE boss still took time to devote intense personal focus on a particular issue or deal when he felt doing so sent an important message or might yield hidden benefits. Deep dives meant "spotting a challenge where you think you can make a difference—one that looks like it would be fun—and then throwing the weight of your position behind it," he later wrote. "Some might justifiably call it 'meddling.'"

Rogers escorted Neupert and Maffei into a corner office usually occupied by Randy Falco, a top NBC executive. Welch was sitting there with Wright and Dennis Dammerman, GE's longtime chief financial officer. After pleasantries, Neupert sat down and explained Microsoft's reservations about the deal. Welch cut straight to the heart of the matter. For him it all boiled down to commitment. He wanted to know that Gates and Microsoft really wanted the deal to happen.

"Basically, Jack was grilling me and taking the test of my character and mettle," Neupert says. "I convinced him that we were serious, that we knew what we were doing and we were going to make this happen, and we weren't dicking him around."

After about fifteen minutes of back-and-forth, Welch finally said, "Okay, I'm with you. I think we should move forward. But I want to get a commitment from Bill along the same lines beforehand."

"Okay, no problem," Neupert replied.

Neupert left Falco's office and within the hour had reached Gates by phone, briefing him on what Welch had said. Soon the Microsoft cofounder was on the line with the chairman of GE, who took the call upstairs in his office at NBC. Amazingly, it was their first direct contact on the MSNBC deal.

Gates told Welch that cable might be entering a slow growth period. Many cable systems were nearly filled to capacity with channels, and operators were increasingly consolidating, making the remaining players more powerful. It was growing difficult to get a new channel into enough homes to make a viable business. Besides, Microsoft had always been more interested in the online side. The TV programming dimension made Gates nervous. "Jack, do you believe the cable forecasts?" he asked.

"I think cable's a no-brainer," Welch declared. "You're the guy who has the tough job with the online part. I don't have any doubt we'll make cable work."

Welch tossed out some guarantees on cable performance that he said would protect Microsoft from losses if the new channel did not get into more homes.

"That's enough for me," Gates said.

It was about 9:20, forty minutes before the press conference in 8H.

When his cue came at the presentation, Gates sounded somewhat wary, at least compared to the superlatives hurled from the NBC side. He stressed that the interactive age was at its "very beginning" and that Microsoft was taking "a long-term view" that high-quality video would become a key component of the Internet.

"This world of new media will require some unique partnerships," he said carefully. "Over the last six months we've been impressed with the depth of news capability that NBC has in its various operations."

For all his meticulously chosen words, however, one would never have guessed that an hour or so before Gates had been haggling with Welch over cable forecasts. Now he summoned up all the media buzzwords of the moment.

"One of the key things," Gates told the crowd, "is that both of the companies are saying, 'We believe in the world of interactivity, but we're bringing this world into broadcast.' We'll be working with NBC to create innovative interactive news content and an integrated media experience."

NBC even flaunted a bit of its technical know-how as Brokaw and Gates engaged in some satellite-enabled chitchat. The pair had developed a passing friendship over the years, and Brokaw noted that they had "informally" discussed a possible NBC-Microsoft partnership "for some time now."

Brokaw asked Gates if, now that they were formally partners, NBC could send him a television set. The joke, of course, was that Bill Gates was famous for his ignorance of TV. His desire to be involved in interactive television was the decision of a businessman, not a fan.

Viewers in 8H saw Gates crack a faint smile. "I promise, I'll watch it," he said, none too convincingly.

Meanwhile, ten miles to the west across the Hudson River, someone was swearing at his television.

Roger Ailes paced in his office in Fort Lee, New Jersey, glancing every now and then at the live video of the MSNBC press conference. His fury was gathering force.

Ailes, the former Republican media consultant who ran the CNBC and America's Talking cable channels for NBC, had done everything in his power to ensure that this day would never come. Although NBC had struggled to keep the project secret, Ailes found out anyway. He was convinced that the mission's code name, The Ohio Project, was a sly dig at him and his native state.

Ailes felt sure that MSNBC was a bad idea. The Internet was still too small to make a profitable news platform, he believed. And because space on cable systems was limited, the new channel meant that something else would have to go, namely, America's Talking. An attempt to marry talk radio with television, the channel was wholly an Ailes concoction. It featured such shows as *Am I Nuts?,* a call-in therapy show; *Bugged!,* in which ordinary people chewed over their pet peeves; *Have a Heart,* a feel-good show about local heroes; and the unfortunately titled *Pork,* a call-in show about alleged government waste. "The lineup really comes out of my head," Ailes explained in one interview. NBC had started AT, as it was known internally, because it felt that CNBC—originally designed to focus on consumer news and business—needed a harder business edge. AT, it was believed, could focus on the soft consumer topics. Management later explored ways to make AT more politically oriented, at one point even trying to persuade talk-radio sensation Rush Limbaugh to join the lineup. "He was interested, but it wasn't possible because he had too many other commitments then," Wright says.

While America's Talking was not burning up the ratings, Ailes felt a deep emotional attachment to it. He was convinced that AT would catch on with time. A few years earlier he had produced Limbaugh's ill-fated expedition into syndicated TV. "I do believe that the niche of talk is the glue that holds America together," he said at the time. Wright remained supportive, too, even when others at 30 Rock were not. "Inside NBC, [AT] was not well thought of," Wright says. "People like their own silos."

Ailes was especially upset that under the new MSNBC arrangement, he would report no longer to Bob Wright but to Andy Lack, which he perceived as a demotion in the corporate hierarchy. "He didn't want to report to Andy, but he didn't want Andy to run it, either," Wright says. "It was just the thought that Lack would have America's Talking, and he wouldn't." In a news release tied to the MSNBC announcement, Ailes was quoted as promising to "lend my support in this transition." But he did not appear particularly supportive at the moment.

Judy Laterza, Ailes's executive assistant, and Brian Lewis, a CNBC publicity executive, watched as their boss's 250-pound frame circled around the office like an agitated beast in the zoo.

"Fuck them," Ailes swore at the television. "Fuck them."

This was a stunning setback for Ailes, who had for the previous two years enjoyed a stellar career at NBC. Wright had first met him years before when Ailes approached him about buying a television station. Wright suggested he think about television production instead and remembered his name when CNBC was looking for a new chief. "It took a little bit of convincing to get him to do it," Wright recalls. But Wright persuaded him that the business channel was a terrific opportunity, and soon Ailes was traveling to Welch's home on Nantucket for an interview.

After his hiring in August 1993, Ailes was soon celebrated at Rock Center for turning CNBC into a credible and profitable network. He filled the airwaves with rough-and-tumble political opinion; one of the hosts he promoted was a brash former speechwriter for Jimmy Carter named Chris Matthews. Another was former tabloid TV host Geraldo Rivera. Ailes personally created CNBC's memorable motto, *First in business, first in talk.* He also minded the bottom line: Under Ailes's tenure, CNBC's operating profits zoomed from $9 million in 1993 to $50 million in 1995. When he took over, CNBC's asset value was about $400 million; two years later the channel was worth more than $1 billion.

Those kinds of results won plaudits at the GE home office. Jack Welch told *The New York Times* in early 1995 that hiring Ailes "may well turn out to be the smartest thing Bob Wright has done in his career." "I was an instant fan," Welch later wrote. "Roger was an edgy and excitable guy, full of opinions." As Wright puts it, Ailes "converted everybody to his own church, which is Roger's style."

But Ailes's edginess also made him a management headache. Upon his hiring he insisted that he report only to Bob Wright or Jack Welch. He quickly began sparring with Tom Rogers, the former regulatory attorney who oversaw NBC's growing cable portfolio. When Rogers made programming suggestions in meetings at CNBC's Fort Lee headquarters, Ailes would retort, "You're a lawyer! What do you know about programming?" In May 1994, on the eve of the launch of America's Talking, Ailes attacked Rogers in an interview with the trade magazine *Multichannel News*. "Tom's had a little trouble letting go because he used to basically run CNBC," Ailes was quoted as saying. "I think he likes to see his name in the paper. . . . Every once in a while, we send a disinformation press release to Tom's office just to keep him on his toes." According to one insider, Ailes ignored Wright's request that he apologize to Rogers.

Ailes also battled with David Zaslav, who sold CNBC to cable operators as the network's head of affiliate relations. Ailes had picked Zaslav for the post over another candidate favored by Rogers, but he soon accused Zaslav of working behind his back on the MSNBC deal and branded him a traitor. By November 1995, when CNBC executives flew out to California for the Western Cable Show, the two were barely on speaking terms. "It was very, very uncomfortable," one former staffer says. "Roger was not speaking to David, David was not speaking to Roger. And here they were, being the face of CNBC."

Ailes did not limit his attacks to those inside the company. In March 1994, during an on-air talk with radio host Don Imus, Ailes ridiculed President Bill Clinton and the First Lady. He suggested that the president was making a trip to New York to "hit on" the Olympic skater Nancy Kerrigan. He noted that of the three lawyers Hillary Rodham Clinton brought to Washington—Webster Hubbell, Bernard Nussbaum, and Vince Foster—one was under investigation, one was forced to resign, and one was dead. "I wouldn't stand too close to her," Ailes joked. White House chief of staff Thomas McLarty angrily called Bob Wright to complain. "Bob and I had a constructive conversation," McLarty told *The Washington Post.* Ailes shrugged off the incident as "a non-issue."

But Ailes was perhaps most pugnacious with journalists. During the 1988 presidential campaign when he worked as a media adviser to Vice President George Bush, Ailes trashed a reporter's television camera because, he said, "I couldn't reach his neck." In the fall of 1993, shortly after taking the CNBC job, he tussled with *Time* writer Kurt Andersen, who was working on a cover story about Rush Limbaugh, Howard Stern, and the talk-radio phenomenon. Ailes, who still had close ties to Limbaugh, decided he did not like the drift of the story, according to Andersen, and during a tense phone call, he asked the writer how he would like it if a CNBC camera crew followed his children home from school. Andersen replied that he wondered how Jack Welch would like it if he knew GE resources were being used to stalk small children. "Are you threatening me?" Ailes roared.

For all the trouble he caused, though, Ailes remained a key player for NBC, and top management remained sensitive about what the MSNBC move might lead him to do. On the other hand, NBC was clearly committed to its new venture with Gates. "I thought the opportunity to partner with Microsoft was a big deal," Wright says. "I was fascinated with the Gates culture. Their vision of the future was very different from our vision. I thought it would do us good to have a partner who was a real leader, a real winner, with a very different view of the future of media and communications than we had."

At the press conference a reporter asked what the new network would mean for Ailes. "Roger's been involved in these discussions for some time," Wright said carefully. He admitted that Ailes and his team would have preferred to let America's Talking develop to its "full potential." But Wright added that MSNBC was "perfectly consistent with the original design and theory of America's Talking." Ailes, he predicted, would "be actively involved in this as it goes forward."

He was already actively involved, though decidedly not in the way Wright wished. Back in New Jersey, fuming at the hoopla on his television set, Ailes stopped short as something onscreen caught his attention. In the front rows where top NBC executives listened and nodded at the glitzy presentation, one of the chairs was conspicuously empty. Ailes and his aides could not be sure, but to them it looked as if NBC, expecting their CNBC boss to show up to his own beheading, had saved him a seat.

2

Television Is Not a Gimmick

"This is the beginning of a whole new concept. This is it. This is the way they'll be elected forevermore. The next guys up will have to be performers."
—Roger Ailes, on packaging presidential candidates for television, in Joe McGinniss, ***The Selling of the President***

One month after the MSNBC press conference, dozens of CNBC employees crammed into a New Jersey studio and gave a boisterous standing ovation to Roger Ailes. For all the headaches he gave his superiors, Ailes's wicked humor and take-no-prisoners style made him popular with many employees.

"Now, look," Ailes joked, raising his hands in an effort to quiet the cheering crowd. "I told 'em you were well behaved. . . . I can't cover your asses anymore."

Indeed he couldn't. As many expected, Ailes had just announced that he was quitting CNBC. He would not be at all "actively involved" in NBC's new cable news network. He introduced Bob Wright, who looked a bit like a college dean who had just stumbled into a wild fraternity party. Emerging from backstage, Wright looked down and barely broke stride when shaking hands with his departing executive. He had come across the river to assure CNBC employees that their jobs were safe and tell them about Ailes's replacement, Bill Bolster, who would assume day-to-day management of CNBC while keeping his regular job as general manager of WNBC, the network's owned-and-operated station in New York.

Ailes was a tough act to follow. When Wright invited Bolster to make a few remarks, the jovial station manager peered around the studio and cracked, "When Roger came out here, I kind of felt like the guy who shot Bambi's mother."

"It's an awkward day for me," Wright admitted to the crowd. "We obviously have a difficult situation with the transition of America's Talking to Microsoft-NBC. That's not a secret.

"The reality is, in the process of all this, we're losing a very good person in Roger," Wright continued. "CNBC's profit has been increased, its programming has been bettered, its ratings have improved, its economic fortunes have improved dramatically.

"Even in a business where people are getting along, sometimes you have problems, and decisions are made by one party or another, and you have to accommodate that."

Beyond the friendly spin, however, relations between Ailes and NBC had almost completely broken down. According to Wright, Ailes had grown "testy" and was in "meltdown mode" in his final weeks at NBC. While Ailes publicly told his CNBC staffers that "change is inevitable," he refused to conform to the new changes sweeping NBC. "I think they would have given me MSNBC if I had agreed to report to Andy Lack, but I wouldn't do that," he says. The two sides couldn't even agree on how to handle the exit announcement: Ailes wanted a news release about his departure alone, but NBC decided at the last minute to toss in the Bolster appointment as well. "I knew they might pull a fast one, so I was prepared," Ailes says.

Was he ever. Over the late fall, when it became obvious that his days at NBC were numbered, Ailes began making some calls. One of his contacts was an old friend for whom he had done some consulting work in the early 1990s, before joining CNBC. The two men began talking and soon sketched out a deal.

At a hastily organized Manhattan press conference just twelve days after exiting CNBC, a grinning Ailes stood beside Rupert Murdoch.

The Australian-born mogul's News Corporation controlled far-flung media operations all over the globe. Among his holdings were the Fox Broadcasting Company, America's fourth TV network; the Twentieth Century Fox motion picture studio; Britain's Sky News; and the *New York Post.* The business had originally been founded by Rupert's father, Keith, a Presbyterian minister's son who took over the Melbourne *Herald* in the 1920s and turned it into a scandal sheet. Rupert studied at Oxford—or tried to, between bouts of gambling and carousing—and returned to Australia to run the family business after his father died in 1952.

Whatever politics the young Rupert espoused were of the trendy, left-wing variety popular among college students at the time; he kept a bust of Lenin, his early idol, in his dorm room. Over his years in business, however, the budding media mogul grew more and more conservative or at least more populist, although his politics often seemed to stem less from devout belief than from business expediency. Murdoch was an ardent fan of both Margaret Thatcher and Ronald Reagan, and, in 1995, he founded a magazine that became a haven for the American neoconservative movement, *The Weekly Standard.* On the other hand, he was also an early supporter of Tony Blair, and his British newspapers have on more than one occasion gone after Tory politicians. As writer James Fallows dryly noted, "Murdoch seems to be most interested in the political connections that will help his business."

Murdoch is consumed by business, and some of the risks he has taken make rival moguls blanch. "Fortune favors the brave," he often tells lieutenants, typically just before embarking on a negotiation that will test the mettle of even battle-hardened dealmakers. Murdoch's courage had won him many prizes through the years, although a few remained just out of reach. One of those was a twenty-four-hour cable news channel in the United States, which Murdoch had struggled for years to create. No matter what Murdoch did, no one seemed to take his news network idea seriously. People viewed him as a late arrival to Ted Turner's party. In the early 1990s, Murdoch hired former CBS News executive Van Gordon Sauter to establish a Fox news division—and the initiative hardly got off the ground before Sauter left.

Now Murdoch had settled on Roger Ailes to launch his cable news dream. Murdoch had paved the way just weeks before by saying publicly that Ted Turner's CNN was "too liberal" and needed a competitor that would restore balance to TV journalism.

"When everybody says you can't do something," Ailes told reporters, "somehow you get up the next day and you find out Rupert Murdoch did it."

Murdoch noted that the Fox broadcast operation was already spending $30 million a year on a kind of loose network news operation. He figured that an all-news channel would spend about $100 million in annual operating costs.

Echoing Murdoch's complaint about CNN, Ailes said the new channel would restore balance to TV news. Studies had shown that Americans had little faith in news organizations and believed bias was rampant in journalism. "Our job is to be objective, to do fine journalism," Ailes said. "We'd like to restore objectivity where we find it lacking."

On the other hand, Ailes admitted that some critics might find that hard to believe, especially given his background.

In January 1968, Richard Nixon showed up for a guest appearance on *The Mike Douglas Show.* Aiming for a political comeback, the former vice president needed publicity for his Republican presidential campaign.

He had come to the right place. Douglas was the Oprah Winfrey of his time. Nationally syndicated from KYW, a Westinghouse station in Cleveland (later Philadelphia), his daytime talk-variety show was one of the most popular programs on television, said to have more total viewers than *The Tonight Show with Johnny Carson*. Douglas specialized in light banter, sometimes a song or a little soft-shoe, with eclectic guests (an early sample lineup: Bob Hope, Marvin Gaye, Tab Hunter, and The Amazing Kreskin). The host was an affable and handsome former big-band singer who in the waning days of the swing era had a couple of hits with Kay Kyser's Kollege of Musical Knowledge. Each week Douglas would cohost with a different celebrity; one week in February 1963 the cohost was a young singer named Barbra Streisand.

Richard Nixon was out of place in a talk-show environment; he was a policy drone, the sort of man whose idea of leisure was wearing shorts with dark socks and wingtips. But his advisers were urging him to try to shake his uptight image by appearing in informal settings. As his campaign against Hubert Humphrey heated up that fall, Nixon would make a prime-time cameo on *Rowan & Martin's Laugh-In*, where he inexplicably turned the catchphrase "Sock it to me" into a question.

The Douglas staff shunted the candidate to a backstage room until it was his turn to appear. Douglas's executive producer was the precocious and flamboyant twenty-seven-year-old Roger Ailes. Chet Collier, the program manager at KYW, had hired the Ohio University grad as a production assistant in 1962. Ailes quickly worked his way up the ladder as associate producer, booker, and backup director. "He had the drive, the energy, the smarts to know what should make the show work," Collier says.

Ailes came from a blue-collar background. He grew up in Warren, Ohio, a small factory town northwest of Youngstown, where his father was a foreman at a Packard Electric plant that made wiring for GM cars. Roger was a sickly child who suffered from hemophilia. At ten he went door to door selling embroidered handkerchiefs that his mother had made. "I was terrible at it," he later wrote.

In college, Ailes worked as the 7 A.M. sign-on disk jockey for the university radio station. He says he landed in television mostly because he didn't know what else to do. After college he "didn't want to do much of anything," he says. "I really wasn't a good student, and I was afraid somebody was going to make me get a job if I didn't do well in television."

There seemed little chance of that. Even in his twenties Ailes had a visceral understanding of the medium and especially of what mainstream American viewers wanted to see. He also had an edgy sense of marketing. In 1967, with anti–Vietnam War sentiment rising on campuses, Ailes concocted an "Armed Forces Week" on *Mike Douglas* that was "meant to give a little pat on the back to our guys in uniform," as the host later put it. Douglas was pictured diving with Navy frogmen, running an obstacle course at Fort Bragg, and being plucked from the sea like an astronaut. The stunts may have been corny, but they earned Douglas reams of favorable letters as well as an admiring phone call from President Lyndon B. Johnson, who invited him to the White House.

So Ailes might have felt justified in going backstage and giving the former vice president a few pre-show pointers. "The camera doesn't like you," he told Nixon. This was not news to anyone who had seen Nixon's nervous and shifty performance during the 1960 presidential debates with John F. Kennedy, but the candidate was having a hard time getting past his discomfort with the medium.

"It's a shame a man has to use gimmicks like this to get elected," said Nixon, who had used his daughters' dog as a powerful gimmick in his 1952 "Checkers speech."

"Television is not a gimmick," Ailes shot back, "and if you think it is, you'll lose again." Ailes believed television was the most powerful communications medium ever devised, and future presidents would win the White House only by harnessing that power.

"To me, it was a media issue, not a political issue," Ailes says. "I was not particularly political at that time. I'm not 100 percent sure I was registered."

The blunt talk apparently energized Nixon. "On the show, he was more enthusiastic than I remembered him to be," Douglas later wrote. "Even made a few jokes. Afterward, he huddled again with Roger before departing."

A few days later Ailes received a call from a Nixon staffer. The vice president had been very impressed with him, the caller said. Would he be interested in coming to talk with the people who were developing Nixon's media campaign?

Eight months later Ailes was pitching a fit in a Philadelphia studio.

"I'm going to fire this fucking director," he said. "I've told him fifty times I want close-ups. Close-ups! This is a close-up medium. . . . I want to see faces. I want to see pores. That's what people are. That's what television is."

Ailes had left *Mike Douglas* to join the Nixon campaign as a media adviser, responsible for managing a series of carefully stage-managed, town-hall-style meetings designed to make the candidate appear more relaxed and trustworthy. Ailes had burned out on *Mike Douglas,* producing six 90-minute shows each week. But what seemed to appeal to him most about the Nixon job was its inherent challenge. Ailes knew that many voters saw Nixon as dull; in fact, Ailes felt the same way himself.

The mission was to make the candidate seem exciting or at least interesting. Ailes believed that not only could television change Nixon's image, but it was perhaps his last hope.

People "look at [Nixon] as the kind of kid who always carried a bookbag," Ailes said in one campaign meeting. "Who was forty-two years old the day he was born. They figure other kids got footballs for Christmas, Nixon got a briefcase and he loved it. He'd always have his homework done and he'd never let you copy.

"That's why these shows are important. To make them forget all that," Ailes concluded.

Joe McGinniss, a young columnist for *The Philadelphia Inquirer,* shadowed Ailes and the rest of Nixon's media team through the closing days of the 1968 campaign, charting their progress in successfully repackaging Nixon for mass consumption. When McGinniss published his account as a book, *The Selling of the President,* Ailes figured as a major character—a profane, intensely driven media wizard with an eye for even the smallest details (in one memo he remarked that Nixon might need "slightly whiter makeup" on his upper eyelids) and an unyielding belief that television could sell anything. McGinniss revealed how Ailes and the other consultants changed public perceptions of Nixon by carefully screening questioners, giving the candidate flattering camera angles, lighting, and makeup, and—perhaps most important—keeping the press at bay. Years later such techniques were standard procedure for political candidates, but at the time *The Selling of the President* was a revelation.

After the book was published in 1969, some in the Nixon camp cried foul, claiming that the author had infiltrated the campaign by claiming to be a graduate student conducting a research project. Ailes, however, did not join the anti-McGinniss chorus, perhaps because he recognized the book's value to his new career as a media consultant. Ailes became a national political player virtually overnight, and he had not yet turned thirty.

"He gave an honest account of things," Ailes says of McGinniss. "I never disputed anything he said, other than the fact that I swore to my mother it was all untrue and I was suing him. . . . My mother was upset that I used bad language, you know."

But the limelight soon faded. After Nixon was inaugurated, Ailes worked as a freelance TV consultant for the White House. The bombastic young media guru ran afoul of the president's inner circle of advisers, most notably Nixon's steely chief of staff, H. R. "Bob" Haldeman. In May 1969, the president wanted a dramatic ceremony in the East Room announcing his appointment of Warren Burger as chief justice of the Supreme Court. Haldeman brought Ailes in to produce the event but was not pleased with the results. Ailes may have understood television, but Haldeman evidently felt he had little feel for presidential pomp. "He blew things pretty well, mistimed 'Hail to the Chief,' forgot the flags on the podium, etc.," Haldeman wrote in his diary. "Probably would have done better without him, but CBS producer was a real nervous type." In December 1970, Haldeman informed Ailes that the White House was getting a new media consultant.

Around that time Ailes went to a party at the apartment of Kermit Bloomgarden, a onetime accountant who had become an enormously successful Broadway producer during the 1950s. His credits included *The Diary of Anne Frank* and *The Music Man,* as well as Arthur Miller's *Death of a Salesman* and *The Crucible.* Given his fascination with television, not to mention his political proclivities, Ailes might have seemed an anomaly among the theatrical demimonde. But he loved the stage—loved the idea of tending to the myriad details involved in putting on a show—and struck up a friendship with the elderly Bloomgarden. Soon they were talking about producing a show together.

"Don't ever chase critics and don't ever try to produce anything the critics are going to love," Bloomgarden told Ailes. "Do what you think is right, what you believe in, what you enjoy."

Ailes, who was still toiling by day as a for-hire media consultant, had some trouble adjusting to his new role as Broadway impresario. Bloomgarden was serving as consultant to an "environmental musical" called *Mother Earth.* Ailes grabbed the reins as producer and pushed to open the show at the Belasco Theatre in October 1972. Closing after just twelve performances, *Mother Earth* was a major bomb.

"My eyes were too big for my stomach, I guess," Ailes says of the experience.

Undeterred, Ailes spent his nights frequenting small theaters in Manhattan, trolling for plays that could be transferred to a larger house. He finally found a likely prospect at the tiny Circle Theatre on the Upper West Side. *The Hot l Baltimore,* by a young playwright named Lanford Wilson, was a tragicomedy about a gang of misfits living in a seedy hotel slated for demolition. "It was an American tragedy that was very funny," Ailes says. He liked the idea that the characters had hit the very bottom but still found humor in their situation.

When the lights came up, Ailes called Bloomgarden to tell him about the play. Then he marched to the box office, where he paid the producers $500 on the spot to option the rights.

Ailes and Bloomgarden reopened *Hot l Baltimore* off-Broadway, at the three-hundred-seat Circle-in-the-Square Theatre in Greenwich Village, on March 22, 1973. The cast included Judd Hirsch and Jonathan Hogan. This time Ailes's instincts proved correct. *Hot l Baltimore* was a hit, winning three Obie Awards for the 1972–73 season, including Best American Play. The production ran for three and a half years.

But the former Nixon media whiz was not destined to be the next David Merrick. Bloomgarden and Ailes suffered another Broadway flop with *Ionescopade,* a musical based on the writings of absurdist playwright

Eugene Ionesco. Bloomgarden's health began to fail (he died in 1976), and Ailes quickly discovered the paychecks in the theater did not match those in television. Besides, he did not like the direction that professional theater was taking.

"I decided that the theater in New York became more about raising money than the creativity of it," Ailes says. "The unions were designating talk houses as music houses. If you went to a certain theater to produce a play, you had to pay sixteen musicians even if it was not a musical. I decided there's something fundamentally wrong with that."

Ailes devoted more time to his communications consultancy, which developed materials for politicians and executives, and kicked around doing odd projects. In 1974, he traveled to Africa with Robert F. Kennedy Jr., then a Harvard undergrad. The pair teamed up to make *The Last Frontier,* a TV documentary about Kenyan wildlife. On his return, Ailes was arrested in Central Park for illegally carrying a .25-caliber pistol. He explained that he was using the gun to protect Kennedy on the trip and had accidentally left the weapon with his camera equipment when he came back to the States. Ailes pleaded guilty to a lesser charge, and his record was cleared.

Ailes decided to return to his television roots. In the early 1980s, he presided over *Tomorrow,* NBC's late-night talk show with Tom Snyder, shortly before it was canceled to make way for *Late Night with David Letterman.*

The onetime wunderkind seemed a long way from 1968.

The vice president was furious. "Tell your goddamned network that if they want to talk to me to raise their hands at a press conference," George H. W. Bush told a roomful of CBS News staffers. "No more Mr. Inside stuff after that."

The agitated candidate turned to his wife, Barbara. "I just had the darnedest interview," he said.

It was January 1988, and Bush, hoping to succeed Ronald Reagan in the White House, had emerged from a brutal nine-minute exchange with Dan Rather on the *CBS Evening News.* The interview had been conducted live at the insistence of Bush's media adviser, Roger Ailes, who believed his client stood a better chance of getting his message out if he was not subject to network editing.

Bush was trying to move beyond questions about his murky role in the Iran-Contra scandal that had threatened to sink the Reagan presidency in 1987. CBS had pitched a session with Bush as part of a series of profiles on the presidential candidates. But as cameras were set up in the vice president's Washington office, a miffed Bush, with Ailes at his side, saw a teaser for the segment: *Still to come, a live interview with Mr. Bush on arms to Iran and money to the Contras.*

On the air minutes later, Rather began firing Iran-Contra questions at Bush, and the exchange quickly grew testy. Halfway into the interview an exasperated Bush pounced, deploying what *Time* later referred to as his "tactical nuclear weapon." He reminded viewers of an embarrassing incident the previous year when Rather stormed out of the studio after a tennis match ran over into his newscast. The network was left with several minutes of dead air, a sin for which Rather's predecessor, Walter Cronkite, said he should have been fired.

"It's not fair to judge my whole career by a rehash on Iran," the vice president said, seething. "How would you like it if I judged your career by those seven minutes when you walked off the set in New York?"

Rather was in fact broadcasting from Miami during the event that Bush referred to, but the precise details hardly mattered. The attack line was furnished by Ailes, who had expected an ambush from CBS News.

Ailes, helped along by the Reagan revolution, had come roaring back as a political consultant. After the dark Watergate years, the fortieth president had made it safe to be a Republican again. Ailes had meanwhile reinvented himself as a kind of Professor Henry Higgins for media-befuddled executives and politicos.

Ailes's theory was that there were no bad communicators, just bad communication habits. If those bad habits could be broken, a speaker could convey his true message and, it was hoped, persuade others to adopt his point of view. This was the secret he was selling to corporations and politicians, a secret informed by all his years of experience as a TV producer, political consultant, and even Broadway impresario.

He summed up the approach in a 1988 self-help book, *You Are the Message: Getting What You Want by Being Who You Are*. "I can't change anyone," he wrote. "All I can do is help them identify and bring out their best qualities, the ones that communicate a positive message." As an example, Ailes referred to a typical client who was "friendly, warm and articulate" in informal conversation but, when a video camera was turned on, became "self-conscious, wooden, dull, uninteresting, tongue-tied and cold." "My job becomes one of trying to get him to change back into that warm, comfortable person he was when we were just sitting and chatting."

When Ailes tailored his media approach to GOP presidential candidates in the 1980s, the results were explosive.

His return to the political main stage was heralded by a phone call from Reagan's staff in October 1984. Although the seventy-three-year-old president was nicknamed The Great Communicator, he had appeared rattled in his first debate against the Democratic challenger, Walter Mondale. Reporters were beginning to bring up the age factor: If reelected, Reagan would be the oldest president ever to serve. Reagan's comfortable lead in the polls was in jeopardy. His advisers thought he could use some help from the man who had helped make Nixon palatable to the masses.

Ailes figured that Reagan, a former actor, was suffering from a kind of stage fright. His confidence was down; he needed a boost. During a mock debate, Ailes was instructed to sit quietly in the back of the theater, where he watched Reagan grow confused as a group of advisers critiqued his answers. When the candidate dispatched one question with ease, Ailes suddenly rose to his feet and cried, "Mr. President, that was a terrific answer!" Reagan smiled broadly and "seemed to grow about four inches," Ailes later wrote.

Aide Mike Deaver had warned Ailes not to bring up the age issue, which was deemed too sensitive to the president. But Ailes persisted. As a White House strategy session was breaking up, he asked Reagan what he would say if someone claimed he was too old to be president. Reagan stopped short. Then he recalled an old joke he had told before to defuse questions about his advanced age. Ailes said that was fine; use that joke and don't say anything else.

Ailes watched the second debate in a room under the stage with the rest of the Reagan team. When *Baltimore Sun* reporter Henry Trewhitt brought up the age issue, Ailes murmured to his colleagues, "Don't worry—here comes a home run."

Reagan said that he had no doubts about his mental agility, adding, "I will not make age an issue of this campaign. I am not going to exploit for political purposes my opponent's youth and inexperience."

Even Mondale chuckled. As Reagan biographer Lou Cannon later wrote: "The only question [in voters' minds] was whether Reagan still had the wit, presence and capacity to conduct the duties of the presidency. For Reagan, the burden of proof was exceptionally light and he more than met it with his inspired one-liner."

Reagan went on to a landslide reelection. Although Ailes did not feed Reagan the memorable line, it's unlikely the president would have recalled it so instantly, and delivered it so effectively, if not for the goading from his media adviser.

Four years later Ailes faced an entirely different challenge. As a campaigner, George Bush often came across as awkward, pinched, whiny—"a wimp," according to some political reporters. He disliked using the word *I* because his mother had taught him that only self-centered people do that. He peppered his speech with grandpa exclamations like *gee* and *darn.* After he scored minor points in a debate against Geraldine Ferraro in the 1984 vice presidential debates, he bragged that he "kicked a little ass." And Bush's WASP background—Yale grad, oil millionaire, son of a famous U.S. senator—did little to help him connect with, say, a factory worker from Cleveland.

Although Reagan simply required some gentle encouragement to return to his homespun brand of humor, Bush was a harder case. Ailes decided that the vice president's image needed a steroid injection. The vice president had to come across as tougher if voters were going to warm to him. Ailes fed him a succession of tangy one-liners which turned up as endlessly replayed sound bites that effectively dewimped Bush. In a 1987 debate, the vice president archly referred to Republican challenger Pete DuPont as "my friend Pierre," a given name that insiders knew DuPont hated. In another GOP debate telecast on NBC, Bush ridiculed Democrats who complained about the nation's problems: "I'm depressed. I want to switch over and see *Jake and the Fatman* on CBS," a detective drama that Bush, who seldom watched television, had reportedly never seen.

But those one-liners stood as nothing compared to the Rather exchange, which signaled a major shift in the give-and-take between major White House aspirants and the media. Instead of deflecting a tough question by delicately changing the subject, pleading media bias, or offering a half-answer, Bush came out with guns blazing against the reporter. It hardly mattered that many viewers were probably unaware of

Rather's tantrum. Other journalists knew, and Bush's outburst served as a warning to them. The speaker may have been the next president of the United States, but the moment was pure Ailes, and it made for great television.

Fred Barnes, writing in the *New Republic,* credited Ailes for turning Bush into the GOP front-runner. "The effect of Ailes on Bush is unmistakable. Not only have Bush's newfound poise and the one-liners fed to him by Ailes thwarted the other candidates; they also have charged up Bush's supporters."

Television had turned the sound-bite attack into a viable—perhaps the leading—campaign method, and Ailes was by the late 1980s the master practitioner of the craft. The erstwhile *Mike Douglas* producer had proven that a well-written putdown could be more than just entertaining; it could actually *persuade.* Conflict sold; Ailes the former Broadway ringmaster was the master of politics as entertainment.

Time referred to the media consultant as "the legendary dark prince of political advertising," even though advertising per se was not his specialty. Liberals grew to hate him; for years after Bush's presidential victory, left-leaning reporters sought unsuccessfully to link Ailes to the notorious Willie Horton ad that attacked Governor Michael Dukakis as soft on crime. (The ad was in fact produced by a former executive at Ailes Communications who was working for a group affiliated with the National Security Political Action Committee.)

Ailes reveled in his bad-boy reputation and gleefully returned his enemies' disdain. Sometimes he got carried away. In the heat of Lynne Martin's unsuccessful 1990 bid to unseat Senator Paul Simon of Illinois, Ailes publicly referred to the bow-tied Simon as "slimy" and a "weenie." "I don't remember being called names like that since I was at a county fair and ran into a fella who had a little too much to drink," Simon said.

Although Ailes worked on other campaigns—including Rudolph Giuliani's failed 1989 race for New York mayor—he had already crested as a political consultant. There was nowhere to go but down. When Bush ran for reelection in 1992, Ailes was conspicuously absent from the president's team.

He decided that he hated politics—was burned by it the same way he had gotten burned on doing six *Mike Douglas* shows every week. "I just got tired of it. It was a pain in the ass," Ailes says. "I was getting older, the candidates were getting younger. I was having to explain too many things. . . . I decided the old role of media consultant was changing. In the old days, you used to be able to win or lose on the candidate's voting record or public statements or strategy or tactics. By the late '80s, everybody was hiring private detectives and doing crazy stuff."

That sounds like an odd pang of conscience for a man who had made a reputation as a political attack dog. Perhaps the distaste for politics' "crazy stuff" is simply a rationalization. Whatever the case, Roger Ailes was set to enter the third act of his wild career.

3

This . . . Is CNN

"When this country collapses, I'm going on the boob tube. And that's how I'm gonna be elected president". —Ted Turner to a friend during the 1970s, in Robert Goldberg and Gerald Jay Goldberg, ***Citizen Turner***

If a traveler leaves Hartsfield-Jackson Atlanta International Airport and heads north on Interstate 85, he will soon see the skyline of downtown Atlanta, visible between billboards advertising local merchants (HANK AARON BMW—A WINNING COMBINATION) and the occasional religious slogan (GOT JESUS? DON'T LEAVE EARTH WITHOUT HIM).

On the southern outskirts of downtown a visitor sees a large open-air stadium. The brick façade summons up memories of Ebbets Field and other since-bulldozed ballpark relics from the early twentieth century. But this is actually Turner Field, the "Home of the Braves," which opened in 1997 after the Atlanta Committee for the Olympic Games retrofitted the Olympic Stadium for the hometown ball club at a cost of $235 million. Inside the park is a museum that includes paintings of Braves Hall of Famers such as Hank Aaron and Phil Niekro, along with a likeness of the park's namesake, longtime Braves owner and CNN founder Ted Turner.

Turner was neither born nor raised in Atlanta (his real birthplace, Cincinnati, seems surprising in light of his southern drawl), but his name is everywhere in the city, and residents feel a palpable tie to him. Some locals affectionately refer to the ballpark as "The Ted," although it was actually in the Braves' former home, Atlanta–Fulton County Stadium, where the dashing mogul routinely rousted fans with "the tomahawk chop." The older venue, where Aaron hit his record-breaking 715th home run, was torn down and paved into an eight-square-block parking lot for The Ted.

Driving about a mile or so northwest through downtown, a visitor will come upon the twenty-one-acre Centennial Olympic Park on Marietta Street, graced by a Fountain of Rings that features twelve-foot illuminated water jets in the shape of the Olympic logo. This park was filled with at least fifty thousand people during an Olympic celebration on a July evening in 1996 when a pipe bomb exploded beneath an audio tower, killing one and injuring one hundred. CNN reporters did not have to travel far to cover that story, because their newsroom is housed in a complex that is literally across the street, overlooking the park.

Amid the redeveloped sparkle of downtown Atlanta's tourist district, CNN Center is architecturally unmemorable. The complex consists of three blocky, mid-rise limestone buildings surrounding a glass and steel atrium. From the street, the edifice could easily escape notice if not for the network's famous red logo affixed to the roofline.

Originally designed as an upscale mall and indoor amusement park, the Omni International failed to lure suburbanites into the inner city and was all but abandoned by 1985 when Turner began a series of transactions to acquire the facility for a reported $30 million. Two years later he rechristened the complex for his rapidly growing twenty-four-hour cable news service.

If Atlanta seemed an odd place to base a global news empire, the location only confirmed to staffers their status as proud underdogs. Turner, the thinking went, was a visionary who realized that New York did not have to be the center of the media universe. News happened everywhere, and CNN was winning because his people got to the news first. "The fact of the matter is you can do CNN in Topeka, Kansas, because of the technology," a network executive bragged to *USA Today* in 1987.

The network remained in CNN Center even after Time Warner purchased Turner Broadcasting System in 1996, and after AOL bought Time Warner in 2001.

Few journalists anywhere work in an environment as bubble-like and self-contained. The network's executive suites, which occupy the bulk of the center's 156,000 square feet of office space, look down on a tourist-crammed indoor food court and shopping mall (CNN T-shirts, mugs, and key chains are available for purchase at the Turner Store). The complex includes a U.S. post office as well as the 467-room Omni Hotel, where visitors to the network's offices are typically booked and where CNN and Headline News play nonstop on monitors in the lobby and bar. During a busy news cycle, executives and reporters have been known to work, eat, and sleep inside the center, going for days without stepping outside to suffer Atlanta's humidity.

"We call it the Biosphere," says Bill Hemmer, a reporter and anchor who joined the network in July 1995 and worked for years at CNN Center. Hemmer, who won an Emmy for his work covering the Olympic bombing, adds with no discernible irony: "I think it says a lot about the network that you never have to leave the building."

Turner himself set an example for cocoon-like working conditions. During CNN's glory years in the late 1980s and early 1990s, the mustached cable mogul sometimes slept on a Murphy bed in his office and would occasionally startle staffers by breezing through the newsroom in the wee hours. Longtime CNN executive Eason Jordan, who started at the network as a twenty-one-year-old desk assistant in 1982, says he had never met Turner until "he walked in the newsroom at four in the morning in his bathrobe to get coffee because he couldn't sleep."

Restlessness is a constant of Turner's enormously complicated personality. Born in 1938, Robert Edward Turner III was the son of a salesman who built a successful billboard company in the South after World War II. Ed Turner sometimes behaved like a comic-book version of an abusive alcoholic; when young Ted revealed that he intended to major in classics at Brown, his father responded with over-the-top sarcasm and ridicule. "I almost puked on the way home today," the old man wrote. "I think you are rapidly becoming a jackass."

Suffering from depression and emphysema, the elder Turner committed suicide at his South Carolina plantation in 1963. His son took over the family business and—despite a legendary penchant for women, alcohol, and especially sailing (he won the America's Cup in 1977 and showed up drunk to claim the trophy)—spent the next thirty years achieving more than Ed Turner could ever have dreamed. The Turner Broadcasting empire grew to encompass a movie studio (New Line Cinema), a major production company (*Seinfeld* producer Castle Rock Entertainment), professional sports teams (the Atlanta Braves and Atlanta Hawks), and the MGM library, as well as numerous cable networks.

CNN was in many ways the bedrock of the kingdom, although it got off to a troubled start. Turner launched the network in June 1980, frantically raising money by selling an NBC affiliate in Charlotte, North Carolina, for $24 million. At the time, cable was just beginning to expand its share of the American television market, and operators were looking for programming beyond HBO. But CNN still made for a hard sell at first.

"The old wives' tale is that the day we went on the air we supposedly were in a million and a half homes," says longtime Turner executive Robert Wussler. "Nobody knows what we had. I don't think we had fifty thousand homes."

CNN from the outset drew scorn and derision from competitors, some of it earned. Its first day on the air was, not surprisingly, an amateurish mess. One reporter, unaware he was on camera, was glimpsed picking his nose. At another point a cleaning lady was seen tidying up in the background of the set. Yet the network started scoring scoops as well. Also on that first day, CNN was the only network to broadcast live images of President Jimmy Carter during a visit to Indiana after the shooting of lawyer Vernon Jordan. The fight with broadcasters turned nasty when ABC, CBS, and NBC decided to deny CNN access to White House pool footage. Turner sued and won in 1982.

While Turner the businessman appreciated that an investment in news could pay off over time, Turner the programmer remained defiantly ignorant about the inner workings of a newsroom. Before the launch, Reese Schonfeld, CNN's headstrong first president, suggested they try to hire Dan Rather, at the time a *60 Minutes* correspondent. Turner, who had never heard of Rather, asked how much he might cost.

"Oh, a million a year," Schonfeld said.

Turner was shocked. "Just to read the news?" he asked.

But Turner the salesman had a special gift. He was charismatic, funny, earthy, quick. Who cared if his pitches were often backed less by fact than fertilizer?

"When it came to cajoling advertisers, he was the best," Wussler says. "He'd go to their office, he'd get down on his knees, he'd get up on their desk, he would regale them. A lot of guys didn't like that routine, but enough of them did to say, 'Yeah, we'll give you a shot.'"

Time was CNN's best friend. Every year had one or two turn-on-your-TV stories, and over time Turner's network parlayed them into distribution and advertising gains. The rescue of baby Jessica from a well in 1987, the explosion of Pan Am Flight 103 over Lockerbie in 1988, the Tiananmen Square uprising in 1989—CNN covered them all, accreting ratings and subscribers and, eventually, profits along the way.

By the end of 1989, CNN had nearly 54 million U.S. subscribers and, together with its sister network, Headline News, an estimated cash flow of $134 million on total net revenue of $291 million.

But that was nothing compared to what followed.

In 1990, Burt Reinhardt told Ted Turner that it was time for a change. Reinhardt was seventy years old and felt that CNN needed some fresh leadership. He had served as president of the network since 1982 when Turner had fired the combative Reese Schonfeld after a series of disagreements. Some network insiders were not unhappy to see Reinhardt go. Never popular in the newsroom, he was reputed to hate reporters, which perhaps presented an occupational hazard for an executive surrounded by hundreds of them. CNN journalists described him as "hermetic" and "a bean counter."

"He wanted no publicity," Robert Wussler says of Reinhardt. "He never wanted to talk to anybody from the outside unless it was a business deal, unless it was making a deal with the Associated Press or [with] television stations that wanted to use [CNN] product."

Turner formed a search committee comprised of himself; Terry McGuirk, who ran Turner's sports division; Gerry Hogan, who oversaw the entertainment networks; and personnel chief Bill Shaw.

The search touched off an intense battle as four internal candidates tossed their hats in the ring. One obvious candidate was Ed Turner, a veteran newsman who was beloved as a father figure by many young staffers in CNN Center and who ironically went by the same name as Ted Turner's father. While running editorial operations in CNN Center, he distributed personalized matchbooks that read "No Relation Turner."

A chain-smoker and recovering alcoholic, Ed Turner fit the stereotype of an old-fashioned, *Front Page*–style reporter and editor. Before he joined CNN, his drinking problem had cost him a job as news director at a Washington TV station. But staffers admired his unflagging dedication to the news: Whenever a viewer wrote to compliment or complain about a story, Ed Turner would park himself at a creaky electric typewriter and tap out a reply.

"I loved Ed. As quixotic as he could be, I really loved him," says Steve Haworth, the network's PR chief at the time. "Ed was always the greatest interview because he was quick, he was humorous, he was a fellow journalist with the reporter who was asking the questions, and that camaraderie was real evident."

Two others who wanted the job were Jon Petrovich, who ran Headline News, and Paul Amos, an executive vice president in charge of news gathering.

The fourth internal candidate was Lou Dobbs. Best known as the anchor of *Moneyline,* a nightly business program that became one of the most profitable shows on CNN, Dobbs also held a vice president title and had authority for all financial programming on the network. After CNN hired him away from Seattle NBC affiliate KING-TV in 1980, Dobbs became a commanding figure in the New York bureau. Smooth and supremely self-assured, he was a superb interviewer and anchor with an unusual mix of intelligence and bulldog charisma. The Harvard-educated Dobbs befriended CEOs, and his program soon became required viewing among the executives, analysts, and bankers who moved money on Wall Street.

But Dobbs was also arrogant and blustery and had a gift for intimidating subordinates and destabilizing the corporate hierarchy. He detested Amos and says he campaigned for the president's job mainly to prevent it from going to a person he felt was not cut out to run CNN.

"I thought [Amos] would take this network down a terrible, terrible path," Dobbs says. "And he was the favorite to succeed Burt."

What Dobbs and the others did not know, however, was that Ted Turner had a wild card. Turner had promised executives that he would pick an insider to run CNN, but a Texas cable executive named Jerry Lindauer called to suggest Turner have a look at Tom Johnson, the former publisher of the *Los Angeles Times.*

Johnson was in some respects like Turner, a gregarious, backslapping southerner. Born into an impoverished Georgia family, he had studied journalism as an undergrad and finished up with an MBA from Harvard. In 1965, at age twenty-four, he won a White House fellowship and worked as an aide to Bill Moyers, who was then President Lyndon Johnson's press secretary. Johnson (who was not related to the president) quickly became one of LBJ's closest lieutenants. He burnished the president's speeches, advised him of breaking news stories, and—according to LBJ's 1971 memoir, *The Vantage Point*—sometimes even served as a sounding board for important policy decisions. It was Tom Johnson who, on the evening of April 4, 1968, handed LBJ a one-line message: "Mr. President: Martin Luther King has been shot." For his twenty-eighth birthday the president gave his aide a gold Rolex watch, which Johnson wore for decades afterward.

After leaving the White House, LBJ installed Johnson as an executive at the Texas Broadcasting Company. TBC was a local station group and cable operator that had turned the former president into a multimillionaire. Tom Johnson became a de facto stand-in and spokesman for the ailing LBJ. On January 23, 1973, Walter Cronkite's *CBS Evening*

News carried video of Tom Johnson announcing LBJ's death to the world. Meanwhile, KTBC, the Austin CBS affiliate controlled by TBC, was purchased by the media giant Times Mirror Co. after the FCC ruled that Texas Broadcasting enjoyed a media monopoly in Austin. Once again Johnson proved his knack for befriending the powerful, in this case Times Mirror scion Otis Chandler, whose family was a California institution thanks to its longtime control of the *Los Angeles Times.* Despite Johnson's scant journalism experience, the dynamic Chandler installed him as editor and later publisher of Times Mirror's *Dallas Times Herald,* then moved him in 1977 to become president and chief operating officer of the *Los Angeles Times,* which Chandler promised would "push *The New York Times* off its perch." Chandler referred to Johnson as the younger brother he never had. Johnson says that he became Chandler's "so-called fair-haired boy." Thanks in part to a financial and population boom in southern California during the 1980s, the *Los Angeles Times* grew exponentially with Johnson at the helm.

Johnson was thus stunned in 1989 when Times Mirror chief Robert Erburu kicked him upstairs to a post as vice chairman of Times Mirror. "I was ousted as publisher in a family coup after Otis was shoved aside," Johnson says. "It was 'regime change.' Later, I learned that various members of the conservative Chandler wing of the board felt that the *Times* was too liberal under my leadership," Johnson adds. This Chandler faction wanted to dump Anthony Day, the editorial page editor, citing in particular his pro-choice editorials. Archbishop Roger Mahony of the Los Angeles diocese personally complained to Erburu that the *Times*'s positions were "ultraliberal," Johnson says.

The forty-eight-year-old Johnson was looking for a way out of Times Mirror when he received a phone call in the early summer of 1990. It was from Dee Woods, Turner's secretary, who reported that her boss wanted a meeting with him. Turner already knew Johnson slightly, although their early encounters were not auspicious. "Ted and I had met once or twice in the years prior to 1990," Johnson recalls. "On one occasion we sat together at a head table in Los Angeles. Ted had been on a rant saying that newspapers would be extinct within ten years. I told him he was wrong, that a strong newspaper would be printing his obituary one day." To prove his point, Johnson pulled from his pocket some figures that summarized the recent financials for the *L.A. Times.* He told Turner the paper was generating $2 million a week in profits.

When Turner spoke in front of the group that night, he repeated his prediction that newspapers were destined for history's scrap heap. But "there may be some exceptions," Turner told the VIPs. "Tom Johnson just showed me the profits of the *Los Angeles Times.*" Johnson spent days explaining to furious associates why he had shared internal numbers with Turner, whose indiscretion and braggadocio had already earned him the nickname "The Mouth of the South."

When Johnson arrived at Turner's West Coast office, in the Century City section of Los Angeles, the mogul got right down to business. "Would you really accept the presidency of CNN, Tom?" Turner asked.

Johnson said yes, although he added that he felt Turner needed to learn more about him. Johnson said he also wanted to hear more about Turner's vision of CNN's future.

"I want CNN to be the best news network on the planet," Turner replied.

"What else?" Johnson asked.

"That's it, pal."

As Johnson remembers it, "The meeting lasted seventeen minutes, [and was] interrupted at least twice by telephone conversations."

Over the next two weeks, Johnson met with Terry McGuirk and Gerry Hogan, who were on the search committee with Turner, as well as Steve Heyer, a Booz Allen consultant hired by Turner to help develop a reorganization plan for CNN. The job seemed to be his for the taking, but Johnson, a painfully deliberate decision-maker, had doubts. He polled his wife, Edwina, as well as a long roster of notable friends, including former president Jimmy Carter, Jane Fonda, Walter Cronkite, Bill Moyers, and *Washington Post* chief Donald Graham. All apparently gave Johnson their blessing.

"After a long walk with [columnist] Art Buchwald in Martha's Vineyard, where Edwina and I had been vacationing with Lady Bird Johnson, I called Ted and accepted the job," Johnson says.

In late July 1990, during a visit to Seattle for the Goodwill Games, an international athletic competition founded by Turner, Tom Johnson was introduced to surprised onlookers as the new president of CNN. "We really wanted someone that had a lot of management experience and had a good reputation as a strong people person as well as strong journalistic credentials," Turner told a reporter.

Some at CNN felt that Ted Turner had taken a flier on someone with virtually no television experience. Lou Dobbs was incensed, angrily storming out of a Goodwill Games reception when he heard the news. He told staffers he was quitting the network, though Turner talked him out of it.

"[I] didn't know who the hell [Johnson] was," Dobbs says. "And neither did anyone else."

The reaction in Atlanta was not much better. "Paul Amos was quite upset, telling me that I was not qualified for the job based on his view that Times Mirror's television stations were among the worst in the industry," Johnson says, adding that he did not have direct oversight for those stations. Ed Turner pledged his support, although he confided to Johnson, "I should have been picked to run CNN."

On August 2, Iraqi dictator Saddam Hussein invaded Kuwait. Johnson had officially been at the helm of CNN for all of twenty-four hours.

"He didn't even have a chance to unpack his suitcase and the Gulf War had started," Steve Haworth says. In fact, the U.S. government's Desert Storm operation against Iraq would not begin for another five months. But Johnson and the other executives decided during that time that war was inevitable and CNN should make a commitment to covering it as thoroughly as possible.

Eason Jordan and Ed Turner planned the war coverage. Senior executive producer Bob Furnad ran the control room, splitting twelve-hour shifts as line producer with Paul Amos. The ill feelings surrounding Johnson's appointment had faded in the crush of the coverage, with one notable exception. "I had a tough time getting Paul Amos back in gear," Johnson says. "His disappointment in not having been chosen CNN president affected his performance badly." Amos quit the network in 1991 and later helped found the Health Channel (he died in 2000).

Johnson realized the Gulf War effort was going to mean enormous costs that had not been anticipated in CNN's annual budget. One morning he went to Ted Turner's office to broach the subject. He figured that between $5 million and $35 million in additional funds would be necessary.

"Ted, how much do you authorize me to spend?" Johnson asked.

Turner replied, "You spend whatever you think it takes, pal."

Johnson recalls, "I walked out of his office and down to the elevator thinking, 'My God, what other media owner on earth would say that?' "

CNN deployed correspondents throughout the Persian Gulf and established uplinks in Saudi Arabia and elsewhere. "Eason arranged with Robert Weiner, our magnificent Baghdad field producer, the four-wire (satellite phone) which enabled us to transmit audio even after the bombs had crippled all other Iraqi communications systems and knocked all our competitors off the air," Johnson says.

On the morning of January 16, 1991, the world learned of the American bombing of Baghdad through the exclusive live reporting of

Peter Arnett, John Holliman, and Bernard Shaw. The impact on CNN was immediate, especially overseas. "Gulf War I was a monumental turning point in our history," Eason Jordan says. At the time, CNN International reached only about 10 million households outside the United States. "I remember on January 17—on the first day after the war started—in one day we picked up an additional one million households in Europe alone," Jordan says. "It was huge."

"I think we pushed the live capability of news coverage beyond where it had ever been," says Haworth. "We were a global news network. . . . [CNN] provided a world access to news [to] some countries that just hadn't experienced that kind of thing before."

Ted Turner was jubilant. His once-ridiculed all-news network was an international brand. And when Senator Alan Simpson and other conservative critics attacked CNN for its war coverage, saying it focused too much on the Iraqi point of view and undermined the war effort, Turner leaped to the network's defense: "You guys just keep covering the news. I'll take care of the goddamned senators from Wyoming," Turner told his crew.

CNN's post–Gulf War euphoria proved short-lived. The Desert Storm coverage had created huge opportunities but also high expectations for the network. Ratings plummeted as the conflict wrapped up in mid-1991. Executives had to consider what CNN would do with its newfound prestige.

A schism erupted among top management, much of it playing out as a poisonous battle between Tom Johnson and Lou Dobbs.

Dobbs, who held a seat on the executive committee along with Johnson and several others, believed the network was not doing enough to capitalize on its war gains.

"Several of us recommended that we put the best-known names from the Gulf War and put them into programs," Dobbs says. He suggested that John Holliman, Peter Arnett, Bernard Shaw, and correspondents Charles Jaco and Christiane Amanpour be put into *60 Minutes*–type newsmagazines that could drive viewers to the network overall.

Dobbs also became a relentless critic of Johnson's management. He was already convinced that the former LBJ aide had too little television experience to run CNN. Dobbs pointed out that the sales and marketing departments—which had reported to Burt Reinhardt when he was the CNN president—reported directly to Ted Turner, not Tom Johnson. And much of the responsibility for news gathering actually fell on other executives, such as Eason Jordan. "The truth is, I think [Johnson] had a lot of good people around him," Dobbs says.

Johnson in some respects left himself open to criticism. He preferred to govern by consensus, which kept most people happy most of the time but could lead to floundering during a crisis. Insiders said that when faced with an important decision, Johnson would gather a group of managers in his office. "Seven or nine were his favorite numbers," Turner veteran Robert Wussler says. "He'd take a vote. And it was always an odd number so he never had to vote. He hated making decisions."

Johnson also had a health secret. He suffered from severe depression, a fact withheld from everyone except his wife and a handful of close friends. He had been suicidal after his removal as publisher of the *L.A. Times.* "I really cratered when I was replaced," Johnson says. Doctors prescribed a range of medications, from Prozac to lithium, with mixed results. By the time he arrived in Atlanta, Johnson was doing better on the antidepressant Effexor, but his symptoms never entirely went away.

Sometimes in his office at CNN Center, "I had to go to an adjoining file room, lay on the floor, and get a half hour to recharge," says Johnson. "I also found it necessary to lay under my desk so my two assistants would not see me in that condition. I did a relatively good job keeping my depression secret. I worked my butt off to overcompensate for any missed hour or half hour, frequently staying late into the night," adds Johnson, who by 1994 was earning more than $1 million annually in salary and bonus. "My mornings always have been my most difficult times, and I did not schedule early morning breakfasts or meetings. Often I would get into the office at nine when I intended to be there at eight."

Turner, who himself reportedly suffered from depression, had at least an inkling of Johnson's problem. Before his CNN appointment was announced, Johnson and his wife went out to dinner in Santa Monica with Ted Turner and Jane Fonda, who was then Turner's girlfriend. Johnson became so anxious about the job that he asked Turner to pull the car over so he could throw up.

As Reese Schonfeld says, "Ted had a habit of taking people who were basically flawed [and putting them] to work for him because they were easier for him to manage."

Dobbs, meanwhile, had problems of his own. In July 1992, *The Wall Street Journal* revealed that he had worked as a paid spokesman for some of the financial companies he reported on, including Shearson Lehman Bros. and PaineWebber. The companies had paid the *Moneyline* host $5,000 to $10,000 a pop to appear in videos touting their services. Dobbs was indignant at the *Journal*'s inquiries, telling a reporter it was "wrongheaded and nonsensical" to imply that his endorsements constituted a conflict of interest.

An enraged Ted Turner wanted to fire Dobbs immediately, but Johnson urged a calmer approach. The network instead "strongly reprimanded" Dobbs and forced him to return the money. The anchor apologized in a staff memo for what he termed "arrogance." Insiders noted the irony of Johnson saving the job of his biggest nemesis within the company.

"I think Tom always felt that should have earned him a little gratitude from Lou, but it didn't seem to," Haworth says.

"Lou was the most difficult executive I ever attempted to manage," Johnson says. "The good Lou Dobbs is one of the nicest, most thoughtful, most intelligent, and most charming people I've ever known. The bad Lou can be mean, extremely critical of others, disruptive, and a bull in the china shop."

When Dobbs urged that CNN put its Gulf War stars in magazine shows, Johnson was characteristically torn. He saw the merit of the original vision of CNN as a kind of video wire that would take viewers wherever news was. But he also understood Dobbs's point that newsmagazines, personalities, and promotion could help drive higher ratings.

Uncertain what to do, Johnson took the dilemma to Ted Turner, who had no trouble making difficult decisions. Turner told Johnson to stick to the original script: mostly breaking news, with a smattering of strong shows such as *Larry King Live* and *Moneyline.*

"Ted felt that news is the star," Johnson says.

Clinging to its roots did not help CNN for long. By the spring of 1994 the network was in panic mode. Ratings had slipped by more than 20 percent since the previous year, and profits were declining as well. That was bad news for all of Turner Broadcasting, because at the time CNN contributed roughly 70 percent of the company's operating earnings. Turner's all-news network was the crown jewel that helped fund his many other ambitions. For the previous year, CNN, CNN International, and Headline News had earned record operating income of $212 million on revenue of $599 million. Part of the problem was that the major news stories of the day—the Clinton health care proposal, the Bosnian civil war, the genocide in Rwanda—were simply not kicking up much interest among American viewers. Insiders grimly joked that what CNN needed was for the United States to start bombing someone again.

CNN executives also carped about new federal regulations requiring cable operators to carry local broadcasters. To comply with the rules, operators were shuffling existing cable channels all over their system lineups, often burying CNN on the dial. "I've been in markets recently where we were on channel 82," Johnson complained to *The Wall Street Journal*.

But the leadership in Atlanta knew that excuses were not going to pull the network out of its rut. Some of CNN's woes had to be programming related. In April, Johnson sent the senior production team a memo asking them to "put the hard-news energy back into the network." CNN needed more live shots and breaking headlines, the memo said. "I want debriefs, eyewitness reports, more crisp packages," Johnson wrote.

Some within the network believed that Johnson was missing the point. Viewers wanted less breaking news, not more. The way to snare a larger audience, especially during slow news cycles, was through interesting features and personalities. The old model of a "video wire service" was not going to work anymore. Viewers were riveted to meretricious scandals such as the travails of the "Long Island Lolita" Amy Fisher and the Hollywood madam Heidi Fleiss. CNN's near-exclusive focus on breaking news from around the world was beginning to look tired and out of step with a post–Cold War age.

A few weeks later, Lou Dobbs and Bob Furnad were deputized to head a committee that would explore ways to improve programming. Furnad was an executive who shared responsibilities for news gathering with Ed Turner.

A rash of "whither CNN?" stories soon cropped up in the *Journal*, *Newsday*, and *The Washington Post*. "The news on CNN isn't pretty these days," the *Post* wrote. Dobbs gave an interview to *USA Today* in which he declared that the network needed more than "Band-Aid approaches."

In mid-June, Haworth, the network's PR chief, was on a three-day Hawaiian getaway when his phone rang at 3 A.M. Ted Turner was enraged by the extensive media coverage of CNN's problems. He felt that Dobbs, Furnad, and other insiders were giving "bad messages to the press," Haworth recalls.

"What are you doing on vacation?" the mogul screamed at Haworth. "I want you back here to figure out how we're gonna stop all this shit!"

Haworth caught the next flight back to Atlanta. He decided to advise Turner to order Dobbs and Furnad not to talk to the press. CNN had to isolate three or four key messages that it would deliver over and over again when reporters called and asked about network problems. The talking points were "some stupid PR-speak," Haworth recalls.

"I had a report on [Turner's] desk by mid-afternoon the next [day], and that day was the O. J. Simpson white Bronco chase," Haworth says. "Our ratings went through the roof, and for the next eighteen months our ratings were escalated by the O. J. Simpson story. I don't think Ted ever read the report."

4

Squish Rupert Like a Bug

"He's kind of like a mad genius. . . . The most dangerous kind of competitor is one who is a little mad, you know?" —Ted Turner on Rupert Murdoch, speech to National Press Club, September 27, 1994

A little over a year after the O.J. chase, a group of executives huddled in a conference room at CNN Center in Atlanta, mired in the details of a difficult negotiation.

Turner Broadcasting System, the parent company of CNN, was weighing a merger with Time Warner, the media giant that controlled a stable of magazines including *Time, Fortune,* and *People,* a major movie and TV studio (Warner Bros.), and one of the nation's largest cable operators (Time Warner Cable), not to mention a minority stake in TBS. If completed, the deal would be worth more than $7 billion and create the largest media company in the world. The combination was designed to foster, in the media buzzword of the age, "synergy"—that is, create savings and promotional and distribution opportunities as redundant costs were deleted and products were cross-promoted through an endless array of TV, movie, and print platforms. But the two sides seemed to have hit an impasse.

Suddenly the startled executives from TBS and Time Warner looked up to see Ted Turner looming in the doorway. He was dressed in a Confederate uniform, perhaps the same one he had donned while promoting Turner Films' epic *Gettysburg* a few years earlier. The mogul known as "Captain Outrageous" raised a saber in mock challenge to the group.

"Get the deal done," he deadpanned.

The Civil War getup was a hallmark Turner stunt, but at the time—the late summer of 1995—the fate of TBS was no joke. The media business was in the midst of sweeping change, with Turner's empire at the center.

Earlier that summer, the Federal Communications Commission—after years of intense lobbying and partisan bickering—revoked twenty-five-year-old rules that had prevented the broadcast networks from forming in-house syndication arms or owning a financial interest in programs beyond their first airing. Among other things, these rules had spurred the growth of independent suppliers of syndicated product, such as King World, distributor of *Wheel of Fortune, Jeopardy,* and *The Oprah Winfrey Show.* The rules also did much to inhibit network growth, because hit series threw off hundreds of millions of dollars in syndication profits.

But the FCC believed that the financial and syndication (fin/syn) rules were no longer necessary to protect viewers from the power of broadcast networks. By the early 1990s, the networks' combined share of the TV audience had dropped to 65 percent, from around 90 percent in 1970. With all the cable competition, network critics had a hard time arguing that CBS or NBC was about to take over the world. With fin/syn gone, the media chessboard looked much different. Giant movie and TV studios could own a network without running afoul of the FCC. The big suppliers could become "vertically integrated"—that is, they could control television production, distribution, and exhibition. Media companies, the thinking went, had to get bigger. So in 1995,

Walt Disney Company proposed a $19 billion merger with Capital Cities, the parent of ABC, and Time Warner and Tribune Company partnered for a fifth broadcast network, the WB.

The options were therefore narrowing for Turner. On the one hand, he was running up against brick walls in trying to get bigger on his own. But if he just sat in his office at CNN Center and did nothing, his empire might slowly wither away in the face of competition from far larger rivals such as Disney. Turner *had* to act.

So the question on other moguls' minds in mid-1995 became: What will Ted do?

The answer would have enormous implications for media in general, and television news in particular.

"They're holding me back, and it just isn't right!"

Turner slammed his fist on the podium during a luncheon speech in Washington. It was September 1994, and the CNN founder was livid that Time Warner, one of the shareholders in Turner Broadcasting, had nixed his plan to buy NBC. The aggrieved mogul told a crowd at the National Press Club that a year earlier he had cooked up a deal to buy the network from General Electric for about $5 billion. "And I went to Time Warner with that, and they said no," Turner said, fuming. "This could mean that I have to sell out," he added. "I'd put my company [up] for sale. That's the only way to resolve this thing—if I can't resolve it peacefully with Time Warner." And whom did Turner cite as a likely buyer of TBS? Rupert Murdoch.

The seemingly spontaneous outburst was a reasoned ploy to shame Time Warner chief Gerald Levin, whom Turner seemed to view as an overbearing parent bent on curbing his freedom. Freely associating, Turner noted that CNN had recently run a story on ritual clitorectomies in African countries. "You talk about barbaric mutilation," he said as laughter echoed through the crowd. "I'm being clitorized by Time Warner!"

Actually, Turner did a good job clitorizing himself. Levin would likely have had no say over TBS's fate if not for a colossal Turner blunder. In 1986, after a failed takeover of CBS, Turner bought MGM/UA for $1.5 billion. The acquisition gave TBS access to a library of 3,235 films, including such classics as *Gone with the Wind* and *Wizard of Oz*. But most analysts believed that Turner paid far too much for the assets, which in any case his company could not afford. Even after selling off nonlibrary pieces of MGM, TBS was sinking under more than $1 billion in debt and tottering on the verge of bankruptcy. Its stock had plummeted to about $17 from nearly $30 a share prior to the MGM deal.

"When I bought MGM, I nearly bankrupted the company, that's true," Turner told the press club. "And I needed some investment money because I didn't have enough capital, like most start-up businesses."

Turner began making the rounds of potential saviors. "We went to everybody: NBC, ABC, CBS," says longtime Turner adviser Robert Wussler. "They were all interested but couldn't quite come to grips with" a bailout deal. Talks with another potential partner, the newspaper giant Gannett, ended in failure as well, Wussler says. That left the cable operators, whose systems aired CNN and other Turner networks. All of them had known Turner for years and understood the long-term value of his company. But these were tough executives with a reputation for driving hard bargains, especially John Malone, the chief of Tele-Communications Inc., at the time the nation's largest operator.

"Ted knew that if the cable operators came in that it would be the start of 'controls' that he didn't necessarily want to get into," Wussler says.

Yet Turner, buried in red ink, had little choice. If he didn't make a deal, TBS might end up forced to shed assets in desperation sales, or perhaps be the victim of a hostile takeover.

A consortium of thirty-one cable operators including Warner and TCI agreed in June 1987 to kick in more than $560 million for a 37 percent stake in TBS. The deal came with the controls that Turner feared. The operators now held nearly half of the fifteen seats on the new TBS board. Turner was also required to get approval from twelve of the directors if he wanted to spend more than $2 million.

The bailout robbed Turner of his autonomy, but he tried to put the best face on the situation. "We had oodles of alternatives," he boasted to a reporter.

Skeptics did not have to wait long for Turner to butt heads with his new overseers. During 1988-89, Turner moved to buy Financial News Network, a start-up business channel controlled by Earl Brian, a physician and decorated Vietnam veteran who had served as California health and education secretary under Governor Ronald Reagan.

Turner believed FNN would complement his growing stable of CNN networks. He argued that if TBS didn't buy the channel, NBC would, and that might give GE enough of a foothold to start its own all-news cable network someday. "We've got to put them out of business, 'cause if they're successful, they're liable to come and grow over into our business," Turner pleaded to the board, inadvertently foretelling the formation six years later of MSNBC.

The operators were unmoved. They worried that the addition of FNN might make Turner too powerful. More important, they feared that such a purchase would provoke complaints in Washington that operators controlled too many channels and were driving independent programmers out of business. That could lead to increased regulation, an outcome the cable industry desperately wanted to avoid.

At the time, "There was a lot of heat on the cable industry from a regulatory point of view," says former NBC Cable chief Tom Rogers.

The TBS board rejected the deal. FNN went bankrupt in 1991 (Brian was later convicted of fraud and conspiracy for trying to conceal losses at the network). NBC eventually beat out Dow Jones in bankruptcy court for the remaining FNN assets, combining them with its fledgling CNBC.

"We merged FNN and CNBC together in the end of '91, early '92, and we were in 40 million homes and fully off to the races," Rogers says.

Turner's fears had come true, but at least in public he held his tongue—for the moment.

"I tried to be a good partner," he said later.

Ted Turner and Bill Gates were watching TV together. It was May 1995, and Turner was visiting the Microsoft campus in suburban Redmond, Washington. Microsoft executives escorted him to a building that was wired as a "home of the future." The house was outfitted with plasma TVs in nearly every room and appliances controlled by wireless networks. Microsoft's Peter Neupert fiddled with a remote, showing Turner how an interactive TV program guide worked.

Soon Gates arrived to join the group. The Microsoft billionaire had invited Turner to Seattle to talk about ways their two companies might work together. Gates had become convinced that Microsoft needed to expand into interactive television, which some experts predicted would become the next major technological platform after the Internet. Neupert had been studying ways to create an interactive news service and was putting out feelers to CNN as well as the BBC.

Turner was, as usual, looking for cash. He hoped that partnering with the world's largest software company would enable him to buy out Time Warner, the people who had "held him back" from buying NBC a year earlier. By all appearances Turner's relations with Time Warner were growing increasingly fractious. A wave of consolidation had whittled the number of cable operators in the TBS consortium from thirty-one to around a dozen. Turner had grown especially uncomfortable after Time Inc. and Warner Communications merged in 1989, because the combined company held three seats on the TBS board. Turner felt that Time Warner had too much power over his destiny. He wanted the company off his back.

The meeting with Gates went well. "Ted was motivated," says Neupert, who over the summer flew to follow-up meetings in Atlanta and Denver with his boss, Nathan Myhrvold, head of Microsoft's Advanced Technology and Business Development Group. Microsoft was weighing a whopping $1 billion investment in TBS. But problems soon arose. The Microsoft executives realized that their grand visions of technology and the future bored Turner. "I don't think he cared a whit about interactive television and the Internet," Neupert says. "It was not what he knew."

Turner was still preoccupied with his dream of a broadcast network. If he couldn't get NBC, he'd simply have to find a new target. "I wake up in the middle of the night sometimes gritting my teeth," Turner told reporters in July. "I'd just beat the bed with my fists. I got no network! . . . It's a source of tremendous frustration." Turner added that he wanted to be a billionaire so that when he died, he could pass on a message to the man to whose high expectations he never quite lived up: "Dad, kiss this."

Turner's obsession spilled over into the talks with Microsoft, which "switched from not only buying out Time Warner but also buying CBS," Neupert says with a laugh. Then that option disappeared as well. Westinghouse announced that it was buying CBS for $5.4 billion. After trying unsuccessfully to join the deal, Turner realized the game clock was running down.

Within weeks Microsoft received a surprising tip: Turner was in advanced talks to sell the remainder of TBS to his old nemesis, Time Warner. If consummated, the deal would almost certainly preclude any role for Microsoft. Over the summer, Turner had surprised everyone by turning from a buyer into a potential seller. Three or four months of media consolidation had left him with little to buy; it seemed like a case of sell or die.

By early September, Gates found himself backing away from rampant press rumors of an impending Microsoft-TBS marriage. Alluding to Turner's talks with Time Warner, Gates told a technology conference in Paris, "We'll pause to let them get on with it."

Meanwhile, as Turner holed up at his Montana ranch, Time Warner's Levin flew to Denver for an urgent meeting with TCI's John Malone. Through its Liberty Media affiliate, the cable operator held three seats on the fifteen-member TBS board as well as 21 percent of the company's stock. Getting Malone on board was essential if the deal was going to come off without a hitch.

Malone was insisting on a number of provisions that made Levin nervous; for example, a right of first refusal to buy out Turner's stake in the merged company. Levin realized that such a right, if exercised, would give Malone a greater than 15 percent stake in Time Warner. Malone, moreover, wanted an exemption from Time Warner's "poison pill" provision that was designed to protect the company from hostile takeovers. If Levin granted the exemption, Time Warner could not issue new stock to dilute Malone's stake and prevent him from gaining a majority interest.

To persuade Malone to drop his demands, Levin opened a bag of goodies at his feet. He agreed to give TCI cable systems guaranteed twenty-year carriage agreements for the TBS networks, including CNN and Headline News. Liberty Media's Encore premium cable network would get an output deal with TBS's New Line Cinema. And

TCI and other preferred stockholders in TBS would get 0.8 shares of Time Warner stock for each share they owned, or roughly 7 percent more than common shareholders.

On September 22, Ted Turner's billionaire dream came true. After five weeks of frantic negotiations, Time Warner announced a proposed purchase of TBS in a $7.5 billion stock swap. Turner would receive an 11.3 percent stake in the combined entity. On paper, at least, the CNN mogul was worth roughly $2.5 billion.

Necessity had evidently helped Turner move past his enmity with Levin. He grinned and mugged for the cameras at a news conference where Levin promised, "This is far and away the dream deal." Levin batted away questions of what role Turner or his top executives would play in the combined company. "There aren't going to be any questions of reporting lines or traditional hierarchies. This is going to be a team and a family that's out to make money and have fun."

Turner liked the part about making money. "I want to see what it's like to be big for a while," he exulted.

TBS employees soon found out what it was like to be big. About seven hundred lost their jobs after the merger was completed in October 1996.

A few weeks after Levin and Turner made their dramatic announcement, Tom Brokaw, in Washington to cover the Million Man March for the *NBC Nightly News,* paused to have a few words via satellite hookup with his old friend Bill Gates. The Microsoft chief, left at the altar by Ted Turner, was visiting the NBC headquarters in Rockefeller Center. NBC executives were furiously pitching him a plan to team up for an all-news cable channel.

For years NBC had been looking for ways to grow revenues at its news division. Like most of its broadcast rivals, NBC News had been bruised by spending cuts and audience erosion in the late 1980s and early 1990s. CNN, meanwhile, had survived its early lean years and was throwing off hundreds of millions of dollars in profits annually.

"For a whole generation of us, for the longest time we all envied CNN," says Andrew Lack, president of NBC News from 1993 to 2001. "They could break stories twenty-four hours a day, and increasingly in the post–Gulf War period in the early '90s [got] the edge on broadcast news as a result."

NBC News had flirted with buying or merging with CNN over the years but could never agree with Turner about how much control each side would have of the combined entity. One of Lack's predecessor's, Larry Grossman, had put together a plan that fell through in the mid-1980s. Now, with Time Warner's purchase of TBS, CNN's fate was decided. If NBC wanted an all-news network, it would have to start one from scratch. The key was finding a well-heeled partner that could share the costs.

"News on cable channels was now clearly profitable," says Tom Rogers. "It was increasingly clear that broadcast news was a huge cost center and that you really needed to figure out ways to amortize that cost over a broader number of outlets."

GE's Jack Welch was an early proponent of partnering with Microsoft. Welch knew Microsoft was looking to expand into television and had failed to make a deal with Turner. It didn't hurt that Microsoft was number one in its core software business and had plenty of cash to invest in a new enterprise.

"Jack loved it from day one," Lack says. "Jack was like, 'Great! Go do it.'"

Brokaw used his star power to help push the idea along. He told Gates that the Million Man March—in which Nation of Islam leader Louis Farrakhan called hundreds of thousands of black men to Washington in an impressive display of unity—was the kind of story that was perfect for an all-news cable channel. *Nightly News* could devote only a five-minute package to such a development, but a cable channel could spend much longer on the topic, directing viewers online if they wanted even more information.

The anchor "was pitching his personal passion, his company's assets, and why he thought a partnership would work," says Neupert. While Gates was skeptical that NBC had the resources to pull it off, he was intrigued enough to continue the dialog.

There was trouble on the horizon for NBC, though. Time Warner's purchase of CNN seemed to set off a stampede of giant media companies searching for their own cable news outlets. In late November, Rupert Murdoch said he planned a "really objective news channel" to compete with CNN. A week later, ABC revealed that it, too, would develop a cable news network. If NBC proceeded with its plans, four 24-hour cable networks were in the offing. Many TV executives wondered if there was room for even two.

ABC entered the game hastily. When news chief Roone Arledge announced the channel to reporters, he offered sketchy details. "I winged it, mostly," Arledge later wrote. "I didn't disclose what the channel would be called or who would head it or how much it would cost—not out of coyness but simply because I didn't know the answers. The one specific I did toss out—that we'd launch in early 1997—was a pure guess."

For all that, ABC still seemed a far more serious contender than Murdoch. For one thing, ABC News already had a huge stable of stars such as Barbara Walters and Peter Jennings, along with such well-known news programs as *20/20, PrimeTime Live,* and *Nightline.* Leveraging those assets across the cable dial could prove lucrative. More to the point, ABC had once before come close to driving CNN out of business. In 1981, the broadcast network and Westinghouse partnered in the Satellite News Channel, which took aim squarely at the fledgling Cable News Network. SNC was offered free to cable operators at a time when Turner was still expecting to get fifteen cents per subscriber each month. Turner was forced to cut prices just when his news channel was struggling to get on its feet. Fortunately for CNN, the ABC-Westinghouse management decided SNC's enormous losses were intolerable and in 1983 sold the entire operation to Turner for $25 million. Turner executives later admitted that if SNC had not folded when it did, CNN would likely have shuttered within a year.

This history gave NBC executives much to think about as they mulled their own entry into the cable news race. By the time MSNBC was unveiled on December 14, senior management at 30 Rock was worried more about Ted Koppel than Rupert Murdoch. "When ABC made the announcement," Andy Lack recalls, "I thought, 'Oh, hell. This is gonna be an interesting competition.'" And indeed it was, although not in the way Lack figured.

Robert Redford and Barry Diller were taking turns teasing Ted Turner. The trio was appearing at a panel discussion at the 1995 Western Cable Show. Redford, promoting his Sundance Film Channel, joked that Turner might have Jane Fonda now, but he, Redford, had had her long before—in movies such as *The Electric Horseman.* "I just like to follow you around and pick up your discards," Turner replied. Diller, the Hollywood mogul who had played a key role in starting the Fox broadcast network, joked that Turner's new role as vice chairman at Time Warner was "not much of a job." Turner cheerfully agreed.

But when the topic turned to cable news channels, the cable mogul grew serious. Murdoch had attacked CNN as too liberal and ripe for a challenge. Turner said the tabloid baron was welcome to try to take him on; others had tried in vain to topple CNN. Furthermore, TBS's new deal with Time Warner gave CNN a significant size advantage. The combined Time Warner would be three times as big as Murdoch's News Corporation.

"I'm looking forward," Turner said, "to squishing Rupert like a bug."

5

An Imaginary Friend

"We invented this business—the economics, the culture, the processes. While it may look easy to duplicate, no one else has successfully recreated what has been built over the past fifteen years." —CNN Communications Plan, 1996

During an internal teleconference on February 1, 1996, an NBC staffer asked Bob Wright what he thought of Rupert Murdoch's new channel, especially now that Wright's old lieutenant Roger Ailes was running it. The NBC president chose his words carefully. "Fox has a history—and I don't ever want to take them for granted—they have a history of making announcements," Wright replied. "I think [Ailes is] the fourth president of Fox News. They have yet to air a program, as far as I know, in ten years (of trying). . . . They don't have affiliates with news. They don't have any structure at all, nationally or internationally, really, to support" the cable channel. "So," he concluded, "it's a real reach."

Compared to some other observers, Wright was being kind. The previous day, a front-page *New York Times* story said that Murdoch's all-news channel would launch by the end of the year but was decidedly pessimistic about its prospects. "With no name and no formal plan for distribution," the article said, "the promised channel inspired widespread doubts about its long-term survival among competitors and cable industry analysts." Noting that Ailes had just been hired as chairman, the *Times* added: "The idea, some suggested, was to give Mr. Ailes a toy to play with, though, given the current state of Fox News as described by some insiders, it may be less a toy than an imaginary friend." There were good reasons for all this skepticism. Murdoch had indeed tried and failed several times during the early 1990s to get a cable news network off the ground, and there was scant reason to believe this time would be any different. The competition was, if anything, fiercer than ever. MSNBC could draw on the formidable resources of NBC News, and the Web site operated by Microsoft promised a key promotional platform. CNN, of course, already had a brand name, recognizable on-air talent like Larry King and Bernard Shaw, bureaus around the world, and video-sharing agreements with stations across the United States.

Murdoch, by comparison, seemed to lag far behind. While News Corp.'s Fox Broadcasting Company owned and operated the largest station group of any broadcast network, most of those stations were much smaller and financially weaker than their counterparts at ABC and NBC. To viewers, Fox meant not news but edgy comedies such as *Married . . . with Children* and *The Simpsons.* While the Fox network had made great strides in sports programming—beating out CBS for the rights to NFL broadcasts, for instance—it aired only two hours of programming during prime time, none of it news. There was no national newscast, no multimillion-dollar anchor. Some of the Fox stations in smaller markets didn't even bother with local news. So there were legitimate doubts as to whether Murdoch's new cable network could even clear enough footage to round out a decent national newscast, let alone acquire live feed of a big breaking story from Jerusalem or Moscow.

If Ailes wanted a competitive network, something more than an imaginary friend, he would have to build it almost entirely from scratch. "We had no news gathering operation," Ailes says. "We had no studios, no equipment, no employees, no stars, no talent, and no confidence from anybody." As the chairman of a quixotic cable network scheduled to launch in eight months, Ailes's first challenge—maybe his most important—was to convince skeptics that it could be done.

Much of that challenge hinged on money and people. How much would Fox News spend to launch operations, and whom could it find to gather and broadcast the news?

Ted Turner had started CNN in 1980 for about $30 million. But Murdoch was not going to get off so easy. Turner's network sprouted with no serious cable competitor and relied on platoons of college kids making minimum wage to get the news out. Fox, on the other hand, was trying to get traction alongside two powerful competitors, one the entrenched pioneer of cable news and the other a joint venture of two industrial giants.

One of Ailes's first tasks was to develop a start-up budget. "I presented three plans to Rupert, what we called high school, college, and pro football," Ailes says. "I said, 'We can play high school, and it'll take us ten years. We can play college ball and we won't have quite the roster, but we'll be respectable and we'll be able to do it. Or you can spend a hell of a lot of money, and I can open a pro franchise tomorrow morning. Ultimately, we settled on the college version in the middle."

That plan called for spending somewhere north of $50 million on start-up costs. That would cover staffing the New York office and the bureaus as well as building sets, buying equipment, and renting office space. But during the summer—as Ailes and his executives struggled to stitch together a news organization—Murdoch realized that the original estimates had been far too low.

"He saw us build it up, and he was beginning to increase assets as we got closer to launch," Ailes says. "He never said no to me on a request for a piece of equipment or a satellite or any kind of an uplink situation or so on. He was able to understand that it was a huge investment, but I think by that time he had the belief that we could probably pull it off."

In the end, Murdoch ended up spending more than $100 million to get Fox News off the ground, and that figure did not include what he spent on getting distribution. Much of that money was spent on getting an army of executives, producers, reporters, technicians, and support staff to round up the news, shape it into something presentable, and then find a way to get it in front of enough viewers to make the channel financially viable. Some of these soldiers—eighty-two, to be exact—came from CNBC and America's Talking. Thanks largely to his success in building CNBC, Ailes had become something of a mythic figure in the Fort Lee office during his two-and-a-half year tenure there, and some staffers had enough confidence in him to follow him to his new gig.

"They all said, 'Oh, great, we're gonna start a network. Let's go start it,'" Ailes says. "I was able to start the network by having 5 or 10 percent of the workforce [made up of people who] worked for me in the past. . . . So I didn't have to try to get people I didn't know and teach them what they needed to know. . . . I [could] focus on getting the network built and then creating enough programming to make it happen."

To help develop programming, Ailes brought aboard Chet Collier, a veteran TV producer who had given him his first job on *The Mike Douglas Show* thirty years earlier. But the new enterprise needed some deeper journalistic bench strength, people who knew their way around a newsroom, who had spent some time reporting and writing and could wrangle the platoons of young staffers who were just learning these things.

Around the same time, John Moody, a bureau chief and editor for *Time,* wrote Murdoch a letter inquiring about a job at his new network. Moody had done well in his fourteen-year stint at *Time,* serving as Rome bureau chief until the magazine decided to close the office and shipped him back to New York. He had worked his way up the masthead and was part of a group of a dozen or so top editors who determined the magazine's contents and direction. But he found himself out of step with some of his more liberal colleagues in Manhattan. Moody was a devout Catholic who had written religious-themed thrillers (*The Priest Who Had to Die*) and was working on an admiring biography of Pope John Paul II (the book was published in 1997). These were not the sort of literary endeavors that won approval from sophisticates at Manhattan cocktail parties.

At *Time,* "I did win one nice battle in 1995," Moody says. "We made the Pope the Man of the Year. That was my suggestion, and I was very proud of that."

Itching to leave print journalism, Moody had put out feelers to CNN and MSNBC, but neither organization seemed interested; he had no TV background on his resume. "My television experience consisted of changing channels on a remote," he says. But Ailes—perhaps because of his own extensive background in TV—was willing to overlook a nonexistent background in electronic media. What was more important was finding an executive with good news gathering chops. He asked Moody to show up for a job interview at 8 A.M., which the candidate thought was a bit early to talk about prospective employment.

"Little did I know that eight o'clock was going to be when he started thinking about lunch," Moody says.

Ailes sat down and began talking. "One of the problems we have to work on here together when we start this network is that most journalists are liberals," he said. "And we've got to fight that."

Moody was surprised by the way Ailes just blurted out such a sweeping premise, especially with a job candidate he had just met two minutes earlier. But he knew Ailes was testing him. "Roger begins a conversation with an assumption, and the assumption leads you inevitably to the conclusion that he wants to get to," Moody says. "You have got to immediately stand up and declare yourself unalterably opposed to what he just said, or else he's got you where he wants you."

But Moody was not opposed to what Ailes said. He, too, was deeply suspicious of the political leanings of mainstream magazines and newspapers. As a foreign correspondent for *Time* in Nicaragua and Moscow, he had grown annoyed with colleagues whom he felt were enamored of the radical chic. "A lot of the journalists were drawn ideologically, romantically, theoretically to the side of the Sandinistas," Moody says. "I always was able to withhold my enthusiasm."

Moody was soon tapped as a vice president in charge of Fox's news gathering operation. One of his first chores was to find a place to put all the reporters and producers who would soon be hired. Murdoch had rented space in an office building at 1211 Sixth Avenue—ironically, right across the street from NBC's headquarters at 30 Rockefeller Center. A record store had closed on the concourse level of the building. Ailes and Moody went down the escalator to visit the space. It was gloomy and had no windows. Moody thought the place looked like the set of a horror film. "I think this is where we'll put the newsroom," Ailes said.

At least publicly, CNN executives seemed nonchalant about the launch of Fox News and MSNBC. "We have new competition," Tom Johnson told the *Los Angeles Times* after NBC announced its cable partnership with Microsoft. "But I will put the quality of our correspondents and our news gathering against any other news organization."

Behind the scenes, however, growing anxiety set in at CNN Center. For more than fifteen years, Ted Turner's network had enjoyed a market virtually free of competition. It struggled badly at first but now was reaping huge profits every year. How would its business model adapt to threats from two, and possibly more, large rivals? Would its advertising base shrink? Would ratings fall? Or would CNN, with its enormous head start, quickly mop up the field and emerge victorious yet again?

Then there was the journalistic side of the equation. For all of its successes, CNN had never been highly regarded for the ambitiousness of its reporting. Rivals granted that the network was very good at covering news as it happened across the globe—which often meant getting a camera crew into a forbidding location and then beaming the results via satellite to viewers at home. That was what made CNN valuable and different. The coverage during the first Persian Gulf War provided perhaps the best illustration of that. But the actual content and style of CNN's reporting were not extraordinary. For the most part, CNN did not offer innovative storytelling, in-depth reporting that went far beyond the headlines, or analysis that changed viewers' minds about important topics. It was, rather, "eyewitness news" carried to its logical extreme—wherever and whenever something happened, CNN's cameras were there. But would that be enough in a world with three or four all-news cable networks?

The only good news for CNN on the competitive front was that one of its prospective rivals had quietly dropped out of the race. ABC, which had announced its all-news network around the same time as NBC, assigned two experienced news executives, Richard Wald and Jeff Gralnick, to work on the project. Within months, however, the proposed channel was scrapped over cost concerns. Financial analysts at Disney, which had recently purchased the network from Capital Cities, projected that the channel could lose up to $400 million in its first few years of operation.

Even without ABC, though, CNN still had Murdoch and NBC to worry about. For all his public bravado about "squishing Rupert like a bug," Ted Turner was worried—worried enough to authorize Tom Johnson to try to lure a big-name star to CNN. This was an important step for Turner, who had in the past famously insisted that "news is the star." In the early days, CNN could get by with no-name anchors and college kids in the control room. But now, Turner figured, it was time to get a big name, someone whose presence would prove that CNN was playing for keeps. "As the new competition emerged, Ted and I saw we needed to bring in some major new guns," Johnson says.

The network initiated secret talks with NBC's Tom Brokaw and Dan Rather of CBS News, as well as Ted Koppel, the respected anchor of ABC's *Nightline.* Turner met personally with Brokaw and joined Johnson to pitch Rather. Each was offered $7 million a year to join CNN, which at the time represented a substantial raise for both. The discussions with Brokaw did not proceed very far; indeed, leaving for CNN would have proven highly awkward for Brokaw, given his high-profile role in the creation of MSNBC. But according to Johnson, Rather was keenly interested. The problem was that CBS had the veteran newsman under an ironclad contract and refused to release him. Rather asked his attorney, David Boies (who later rose to national fame during the government's antitrust case against Microsoft), to negotiate an exit. But even Boies came away empty-handed.

A different problem arose with Koppel. Johnson says the *Nightline* host wanted to lead the CNN International channels and shape the networks' global coverage. Unfortunately, that was the bailiwick of one of Johnson's favorite lieutenants, Eason Jordan, who had risen from a lowly desk position to become one of CNN's top news executives. The ever-loyal Johnson was not inclined to elbow Jordan aside even for Ted Koppel.

With CNN running into roadblocks in its efforts to land a name-brand news anchor, the network began focusing on ways to hone its marketing message. In early 1996, not long after Murdoch announced Fox News, the CNN public relations department devised a "communications plan" designed to remind the industry of the network's achievements and blunt the impact of its new competitors. Much of the plan consisted of positive messages that CNN executives and publicists could parrot back to advertisers, the investment community, and the press.

"CNN has never been better positioned to successfully meet any competitive challenge," the report read. "The CNN brand for news and record of excellence and fairness are well known."

One section of the report addressed Fox News specifically and attempted to rebut any suggestion that Murdoch's channel might prove a competitive threat. The report also took a swipe at Murdoch himself, using his reputation as a tabloid baron to raise questions about his new cable outfit. "CNN's record for fairness, accuracy and timeliness speaks for itself," the report stated. "Murdoch's record in the news business in Australia, the UK, and the US also speaks for itself . . . CNN by all measures . . . is seen as the most trusted news source—especially compared to Fox."

The report repeated the *Times*'s "imaginary friend" gibe but noted that "some add that Murdoch, if committed, should not be treated lightly."

Roger Ailes felt confident that Murdoch was committed and that Murdoch was correct when he said that a large portion of the American public had been cast aside by mainstream news organizations, including CNN. Ailes believed a new twenty-four-hour news channel could work because these viewers were hungering for an alternative to what they viewed as biased liberal coverage. Conservatives could vent their frustrations on talk radio, but the rest of the media often ignored or ridiculed their views.

Ailes felt certain he knew how to reach these disenfranchised viewers. The vocal minority that populated many call-in radio shows were in many respects similar to the "silent majority" Ailes had pursued for Nixon during the turbulent '60s. Before the Fox News launch, Ailes hired a Democratic pollster to look at Americans' perceptions of the media. "Somewhere between 65 and 75 percent of the American people believe the media tipped to the left," Ailes says. "Now whether it does or it doesn't, if that's what they believe, that leaves a lot of room as long as you don't tip to the right. As long as you continue to let the liberals say what they want but balance it with somebody who doesn't agree with it, you're going to open it up."

Critics argued that tipping to the right is exactly what Fox News did. Ailes, not surprisingly, doesn't see it that way. "We just broadened the dialog and broadened the debate. That allowed us to get a foothold because nobody had ever seen that before. The only conservative to ever do television prior to [Fox News] was [columnist] Bob Novak. So there were four hundred liberals and Bob Novak. The public knew that."

Some of this is pure exaggeration. Plenty of conservatives held forth on the airwaves before Fox News came along. Columnist William F. Buckley Jr., for example, began hosting the PBS debate show *Firing Line* thirty years before Fox News premiered. Yet in tackling the issue of alleged media bias, Ailes was doing more than just exploiting an untapped market. He was addressing one of the most divisive and sensitive topics in television journalism. Ailes himself devised the network's two memorable promotional slogans, "Fair and Balanced" and "We Report, You Decide," which cut to the heart of the debate over media bias. Both mottos operated as important signals for conservative viewers. By advertising its supposed objectivity, Fox was attacking perceived bias in rival news organizations. The mottos also alerted viewers that Fox would offer a different perspective from, say, CBS or CNN. Inside Fox News, "fair and balanced" over time became a winking synonym for "conservative," as in, *I know that congressman likes our network, because he's fair and balanced.*

As Tim Graham wrote in *National Review Online,* "Fox's founding declaration of difference was to announce the slogan 'We report, you decide.' This is a shocking deviation from the liberal media modus operandi, which is marinated in the impatient belief that the American people are too politically unreliable to be allowed to make decisions for themselves. With that slogan in the air, liberal media critics like the *Co-*

lumbia Journalism Review quickly announced the discovery of a media-bias problem—but only at Fox."

Fox staffers got a quick taste of what happens when a news organization advertises itself as a corrective to the liberal media. Some of the problems were common to any start-up. At launch, Fox News had lined up only 17 million subscribers, or less than one-fifth of the nation's TV households. That made it difficult to persuade Washington press aides that it was worth their bosses' time to show up and kick around the issues of the day. "We were trying to get people from the White House . . . leaders in the Senate, in the House," producer Bill Shine says, "And they're looking at us [saying], 'You're not even on in our guy's district.'"

But there was something else working against Fox as well. Moody was hoping to persuade President Clinton to make an on-camera appearance for Fox's launch. This was not an idle dream. Clinton had agreed to an interview with Tom Brokaw when MSNBC launched in July. The event drew eight thousand questions to the president over the Internet and generated dozens of mentions in major newspapers. Moody traveled to Washington to make his pitch to George Stephanopoulos, who was then a senior policy adviser to Clinton.

"He came on MSNBC, and we're hoping that he'll come on Fox," Moody told Stephanopoulos. The Clinton aide began laughing. Moody, somewhat embarrassed, asked, "Why wouldn't he?"

Stephanopoulos sighed. "Well, for one thing, MSNBC's not owned by Rupert Murdoch and run by Roger Ailes," he said.

On September 3, 1996, hundreds of Fox News staffers crowded into a conference room at the New York Hilton, just up Sixth Avenue from network headquarters. The event was billed as an orientation session for new employees, although it seemed more like a pep rally. Over the summer, Ailes, Collier, and Moody had hired nearly one thousand staffers, most of them young and relatively inexperienced. The network had prepared short videotapes designed to pump up the crowd. One tape bragged that Fox had already built the largest network-owned and -operated station group and won the rights to NFL, NHL, and major league baseball games, and so starting a successful news network would be a cinch. The pitch ended with the slogan "Fox can." Another tape featured a montage of Fox News' reporters and personalities, set to the tune of "Something's Coming" from *West Side Story.* A few of the faces were familiar—Bill O'Reilly, for instance, had served as anchor for the syndicated tabloid show *Inside Edition,* and Catherine Crier had worked for CNN and ABC News—but most were young unknowns, such as Sean Hannity and Rita Cosby. Doug Kennedy, hired as a reporter, was recognized less for his journalistic bona fides than for being the son of the late Senator Robert F. Kennedy.

Ailes did his best to whip up morale. "You guys are at the beginning of history here," he told the crowd. "Fox News is gonna be around for decades."

But the attendees soon got a taste of Ailes's more outrageous side. At one point, he made little speeches introducing the network's other top executives, who had joined him onstage. While introducing a female attorney who worked in legal affairs, he paused and faced the crowd. "You know the difference between lawyers and prostitutes?" Ailes asked. "Lawyers keep doing you even after you're dead."

Nervous laughter fluttered through the room.

"It was such an over-the-top joke," recalls one Fox employee who was there. "I mean, PC be damned."

As time went on, though, much of the joking and cockiness faded away. Launch was in just a few weeks, and to Ailes the Fox staff looked woefully unprepared to take on a strong local news team, let alone

CNN. He became increasingly unhappy with what he saw taking place in the studio. During practice runs, the anchors seemed shifty and befuddled. The sets looked cheap. Some of the less experienced reporters got tongue-tied on camera. And there were frequent technical miscues, such as dropped audio and TelePrompTer glitches.

On September 30, Ailes sent a single-spaced, four-page memo to the senior production staff. The memo revealed his attention to even the most minor studio details—first glimpsed nearly thirty years earlier when he was producing promotional broadcasts for the Nixon campaign—as well as his aggressive management style.

"I arrived in the control room at 5:50 A.M. today," the memo began. "Apparently at 5:30 A.M. the producer intercom was checked out. At 5:55 A.M. in the control room we had total chaos because the producer could not talk to the talent. The talent was left blind on the set and no one could figure out what the heck was going on. Engineering, please fix this immediately. More importantly, why did it happen?"

Ailes then proceeded, in stream-of-consciousness fashion, to tick off a list of flaws that staffers needed to address immediately.

"There is too much orange in our promos and graphics. I don't want to look like the Halloween network. Start cutting back on orange. . . . The set behind the anchors in studio A looks like a housing project. We spent a million dollars on sets; what the heck is going on? I don't want to hear that it's not finished. We're launching in less than a week. . . . Everybody on camera looks greasy and hot. . . . Tell [anchors] Gordie Hershiser and Louis Aguirre to wear neckties with a little more color in them. They look like funeral directors. . . . Something's distracting [anchor] Alison Costarene. Her eyes keep darting around from side to side. . . . We still appear to be having some problems with TelePrompTer [sic]. . . . If the prompter jams and the anchor freezes, what are your plans?"

The memo concluded with an appeal to work harder, even though some staffers were already working so many hours they checked into midtown hotels to cut down their commute times.

"Nobody in this news organization should be on less than a 12-hour day until a month after launch. *That's just the way it is.* If you wanted some other line of work, you could get a job across the street in a shoe store. I think they're on 8-hour shifts."

Ailes was still not convinced, however, that he had driven home his point. He felt the need to do something more dramatic, so he called for a meeting of top staffers on October 2—at 4 A.M. Ailes knew that most of the staffers would be up late the night before at a Fox News launch party attended by Murdoch, New York mayor Rudolph Giuliani, and other VIPs.

"The party ends at 10 P.M., and there was an employee party after that, starting at about 11," recalls one Fox executive. "We all got back to the hotel at 1 A.M. No one slept because they were afraid not to be there at 4 A.M."

As it happened, the meeting *was* the message. Ailes had drawn a technique from the drill sergeant's playbook, forcing senior staff to show up at the office before dawn on less than three hours' sleep. But the gathering itself lasted only forty-five minutes and seemed somewhat anti-climactic. Ailes simply stressed how important it was to launch on time October 7. "We can either drop the ball for Rupert and be embarrassed, or we can make history," he said.

Early on the morning of October 7, Fox News greeted the world—or at least the tiny fraction of it that bothered to tune in. Anchors Louis Aguirre and Alison Costarene were the first to appear on-screen. "It's

6 A.M. in the East. Welcome to Fox News," Aguirre announced. Costarene then began reading a news story.

Moody watched in the control room. "Talk about starting under the radar," he remembers thinking.

In the days before launch, other media had in fact begun to pay some attention to Fox News. *Newsweek* pitched a Fox versus MSNBC story, but Ailes declined to participate. "I think we're gonna lay low," he told his executives. He believed MSNBC's splashy launch had set up overly high expectations for the channel, and he did not want to make the same mistake.

In truth, Fox faced little danger of media overkill. News Corp had been unable to secure distribution in Manhattan, so most of the major TV writers couldn't see what Ailes was up to even if they wanted to. On launch day, the PR department had to invite critics from the Associated Press and other organizations over to Fox's Sixth Avenue office so they could write their reviews.

The premiere came off without any major embarrassments; in fact, Fox even landed a few scoops. The channel revealed that Palestinian leader Yasser Arafat would make a state visit to Israel. There was no Clinton interview, but Catherine Crier did conduct a lengthy chat with GOP presidential candidate Bob Dole, who was lagging badly in the polls and needed all the publicity he could get. "She turned in as good a job of questioning the man as I have seen on television," Walter Goodman wrote in *The New York Times*. "Crier pressed him for almost twenty minutes on economics, drugs, tobacco, welfare, and other subjects."

But there were enough gaffes to confirm Ailes's suspicion that many Fox News staffers needed more seasoning before they were ready to topple CNN. The big "get" for the premiere was anchor Mike Schneider's live interview with Israeli prime minister Benjamin Netanyahu.

Viewers probably would have been more impressed if a satellite glitch had not killed the prime minister's audio during the middle of the broadcast. "Thankfully we were only in 17 million homes back then," Shine says, "because we could make mistakes and people were like, 'Okay.' "

At 9 P.M., Sean Hannity was joined by a liberal sidekick, Alan Colmes, in a show that the *Times* described as "a *Crossfire* copycat." Shine, who produced the show, remembers that the first few efforts were indeed uninspiring. "Every October we try to pull out the first *Hannity and Colmes* and run a clip of it, and every year Sean is, like, 'I don't want to see that,' " Shine says. "It just looks bad. They were just green. [There were] tape problems, chyrons [the graphics that identify guests] being wrong, names misspelled. You booked a guest to come on and talk about politics, and they didn't know anything about politics."

The newspaper reviews were generally respectful, although hardly effusive. The *Times* noted that Fox was merely another entrant in a three-way cable news race and remarked that a big breaking story would offer the true test of its mettle. "The Fox producers appear to be going for a youthful look, a brisk pace and a direct approach: young reporters, fast-moving pictures, colloquial comments," the *Times* wrote.

Matt Roush of *USA Today* was decidedly unimpressed, calling the Fox News launch "handsome but humdrum." "For now," he concluded, "CNN won't lose any sleep."

6

Fair and Balanced

"There is no conspiracy whatever in network news departments. What we are seeing is: power lust." —Edith Efron, *The News Twisters*

When Roger Ailes hired a Democratic pollster to look at Americans' perceptions of the media, he was tapping into a source of deep anger for many viewers.

Conservative critics have suffered no shortage of surveys that point to leftist bias in the news media. *The Media Elite,* a widely quoted 1980s study of opinion at leading networks and publications, found that 81 percent of the 240 journalists interviewed voted Democratic in every presidential election from 1964 to 1976. A 1995 poll by the Times Mirror Center (later Pew Research Center) for the People and the Press determined that only 5 percent of journalists surveyed identified themselves as conservative, compared to 40 percent of the American public.

The suspicion among a majority of Americans is that journalists' opinions seep into their coverage, and Ailes argues that in this instance perception is just as important as reality. An August 2002 poll by the Pew Center found that 59 percent of respondents believe that news organizations are politically biased. Sixty-seven percent said that news organizations try to cover up rather than admit their mistakes. And 58 percent said the news media get in the way of society's solving its problems.

"If you talk to journalists who cover Washington," says Fox News's Brit Hume, "you won't find very many who are pro-life, you won't find very many who are environment movement skeptics, you won't find very many who think that the NRA's anything other than a menace. You will find very few who are Republicans, and you won't find very many who are self-acknowledged conservatives. It's just not there."

In seeking to redress this imbalance, Fox News had, as Ailes suspected, a ready-made audience. Many viewers had been waiting for an antinetwork network, for the problem of bias in TV news is almost as old as TV news itself.

For many years newly hired producers at CBS News received a looseleaf notebook bulging with typewritten procedures and memos. This was the News Standards handbook, authored by a former attorney named Dick Salant. Employees were asked to sign an affidavit promising that they would read and abide by the rules in the handbook.

Salant, president of CBS News through much of the 1960s and '70s, was probably the person most responsible for standardizing fairness and ethics in broadcast news. His handbook stipulated strict ethical guidelines for producers and reporters. News staffers were not permitted to work in any sort of entertainment venture. Postproduction music and sound effects were banned from news programs. Dramatic "reenactments" were taboo, and every taped interview was subject to rigid editing policies designed to ensure fairness. His standards undoubtedly drained some of the juice from TV reporting, Salant confessed, "but that is the price we pay for dealing with fact and truth." The standards were so deeply ingrained that anchor Walter Cronkite ordered that any opinionated commentary piece from contributor Eric Sevareid run as the next to last rather than the last item on the *CBS Evening News.* Every night Cronkite signed off with "And that's the way it is," and he did not want viewers to think that his tag line somehow endorsed a Sevareid opinion that directly preceded it.

Although Salant was not trained as a journalist, he became the principal protector of TV news's integrity and ethics, and many of his standards were followed by other networks as well. Under his watch, CBS became the country's undisputed number one news network; it expanded the evening newscast from fifteen minutes to a half hour, tapped Cronkite as the anchor, inaugurated a full-time unit to cover elections, opened numerous bureaus, and created the documentary series *CBS Reports* as well as the pioneering newsmagazine *60 Minutes.* Yet, as Peter J. Boyer wrote, "Those things might have happened under another executive. Dick Salant's contribution to a CBS News that was defining itself in the unfolding television age was something infinitely more valuable: He gave it character."

But Salant's emphasis on fairness and objectivity did not inoculate CBS News from charges of bias. On the contrary, it only gave fodder to critics who accused the network of failing to meet its own high standards. In February 1971, for example, CBS aired a one-hour documentary, *The Selling of the Pentagon,* which cast a harsh light on various public-relations strategies employed by President Nixon's Defense Department. Outraged Pentagon officials accused CBS of distorting facts and, ironically, manipulating interviews through deceptive editing. The outcry led to congressional hearings and a subpoena for outtakes from the CBS program.

The type of journalism practiced by CBS News during the '60s remained a favorite target of conservative critics even after Salant's retirement in 1979. In 1985, both Cronkite and Salant defended the network against a *Wall Street Journal* editorial that accused the network of biased reporting in the wake of the Tet offensive seventeen years earlier and criticized CBS for institutionalizing a style of journalism that misled viewers by mixing fact and opinion. In a letter, Salant alluded to "the longstanding policy at CBS that there should be no intermingling of factual reporting and personal editorialization." But by that time the media's liberal bias had already become an article of faith, thanks largely to a magazine writer who believed the TV news business was helping tear the country apart.

Edith Efron smelled a rat in the 1968 presidential race. She was persuaded that network TV's coverage of the campaign had been tainted by liberal bias. The fact that Nixon had won anyway did not alter her views.

As a staff writer for *TV Guide* during the 1960s, Efron wrote some deadly serious profiles of small-screen celebrities; a two-part 1969 profile of Raymond Burr, for instance, depicted the *Ironside* actor as a tormented "caldron of frustrations." Efron, it turned out, was brewing some frustrations of her own. Interested in the byplay of politics and mass media, she won a grant from the Historical Research Foundation and donned the mantle of social scientist, applying the quantitative methods in vogue at the time to arrive at an extensive theory of television news bias.

She published her results as *The News Twisters* (1971), perhaps the first book-length critique of alleged political one-sidedness in broadcast journalism. Efron conceded that the First Amendment allowed print reporters to be as biased as they pleased. But the situation was far different for broadcast television, she argued, which was by the late 1960s where most Americans got their news. Since 1949—the dawn of commercial television—the Federal Communications Commission had mandated the so-called fairness doctrine, which required broadcasters to "afford reasonable opportunity for the discussion of conflicting views of public importance." In practice this meant that broadcasters were supposed to air opposing sides of controversial topics. The Supreme Court upheld the constitutionality of the fairness doctrine in 1969. As Efron put it, "*Broadcast news is explicitly denied the First Amendment right to be biased*" (italics in original).

So Efron went on a bias hunt. Her researchers recorded and transcribed the nightly newscasts of ABC, CBS, and NBC from September 16 to November 4, 1968—the six-week period when the presidential campaign was in full swing. Each transcript ran more than one hundred thousand words. Efron then indexed the material by subject (the presidential campaign, the Vietnam War, "violent radicals") and combed the text for opinion, which she defined as any passage in the transcript "which communicates the pro or con views of an individual or group" on a certain controversial topic. Needless to say, Efron's determination of what constitutes an opinion is open to debate (for example, does a reporter's use of the word *heckler* to describe someone who disrupts a political speech serve as an expression of opinion?).

Armed with her statistics, Efron found liberal bias sprouting everywhere in television news. The vast majority of opinion aired about Nixon was against the candidate, she reported, while his Democratic challenger, Hubert Humphrey, enjoyed far more support. The networks had also slanted their coverage against the U.S. policy in Vietnam, promoted the cause of black militants, and largely ignored the problems caused by violent radicals, Efron found.

In many respects, time has been unkind to *The News Twisters.* The statistical polemics favored by the author have largely fallen out of favor, at least in popular debate. More problematic is that the fairness doctrine, which Efron relied upon to develop her definition of bias, was rescinded by President Reagan's FCC in 1987. The doctrine had been attacked for years by both conservatives, who argued that it constituted an unwarranted governmental intrusion into station policies, and liberals, who worried that the rule encouraged broadcasters to avoid controversial topics and thus quashed free speech. Subsequent efforts to revive the doctrine have proven futile.

But Efron's book influenced such media critics as Accuracy in Media's Reed Irvine and L. Brent Bozell III, founder of the conservative watchdog Media Research Center, and helped codify the notion of a TV news culture awash in liberal bias. As economist Daniel Sutter wrote in the *Cato Journal* in 2001, "The documentation of media bias has become something of a cottage industry since Edith Efron's pioneering study." TV executives were predictably scornful of Efron's methods, but even they did not dispute her influence. Efron "started the whole process of saying the press is liberal and used very suspect research to prove her points," says former ABC News executive Richard Wald. "It just kept growing from there. I think she was the first to [examine alleged bias] in a pseudo-scientific way. . . . It was very politically motivated and it began a whole wave of those things."

Efron was indeed something of a prophet, a conservative Cassandra. She bemoaned the gap between the liberal elites who ran the New York media and the rest of the country. That gap resulted in "explosions of anger by millions, even the majority, of Americans over network coverage." If the situation persists, she added, "one can expect repeated groundswells of rage." It's not too much of a stretch to see such a prediction encompassing the rise of angry talk-radio conservatives such as Rush Limbaugh and Michael Savage.

In a 1984 speech before the National Conservative Foundation, Ted Turner sounded like an Edith Efron disciple. The "greatest enemies" of the nation, Turner thundered, were "the three television networks and the people who run them." The networks were "constantly tearing down everything that has made this country great." To Turner intimates, the speech was not surprising at the time. The CNN founder had started his business career as a staunch conservative with a strong anti–news media streak. Indeed, he told associates that he grew up hating the press because his father, the South Carolina billboard magnate Ed Turner, would often bring home an armload of papers filled with editorials attacking outdoor signage for cluttering the southern landscape.

In the mid-1980s, Senator Jesse Helms announced a campaign to end the liberal bias at CBS by encouraging conservatives to buy stock in the parent company. Turner reportedly met with Helms and his associates and briefly considered joining their effort.

Yet conservatives quickly realized that Turner was not the media savior for whom they had been searching. Ever the opportunist, he appeared to have seized upon the Helms agenda to advance his own (ultimately unsuccessful) bid to buy CBS. Moreover, during the second half of the 1980s—culminating with his courtship and marriage of actress Jane Fonda—the mogul Turner appeared to undergo a political conversion. He began speaking out in favor of liberal causes and tapped his growing fortune to subsidize an ambitious save-the-world agenda. In 1986, he started the Goodwill Games, an international athletic contest, as a means of reducing Cold War tensions. Conservatives attacked the move as pro-Soviet propaganda.

By 1990, Turner had begun celebrating CNN's role as a force for global change—a point that was anathema to conservatives suspicious of globalism. "I wanted to use communications as a positive force in the world, to tie the world together," Turner told *The Wall Street Journal*. "And you know something, it's working."

During Gulf War I, CNN's liberal bona fides were fixed in the f many conservatives. Peter Arnett's reporting, in particular, was attacked as relentlessly skeptical of U.S. policy and biased toward Iraqis. Reed Irvine's Accuracy in Media gave Arnett "the Saddam Hussein Prize for Propaganda."

By the time Fox News was launched, the crusade against supposed left-leaning bias in TV had hit a high point. In February 1996, just eight months before Fox appeared, *The Wall Street Journal* published an op-ed piece headlined NETWORKS NEED A REALITY CHECK. The article began: "There are lots of reasons fewer people are watching network news, and one of them, I'm more convinced than ever, is that our viewers simply don't trust us. And for good reason." The author, Bernard Goldberg, argued that liberal bias "comes naturally to most reporters." His piece went on to attack as egregiously unfair a *CBS Evening News* segment that had called Republican presidential candidate Steve Forbes's flat-tax proposal "wacky."

Goldberg was not just another disgruntled media critic but a veteran TV correspondent who had joined CBS News in 1972, the apex of the Dick Salant years. His jeremiad understandably caused an internal uproar at CBS and ultimately led to his departure from the network four years later. He later expanded his criticisms into a book, *Bias: A CBS Insider Exposes How the Media Distort the News.* Goldberg argued that network news staffers did not intend to be biased; rather, they operated under a largely unspoken system of values and shared assumptions that inadvertently resulted in slanted coverage.

Journalism "elites are hopelessly out of touch with everyday Americans," Goldberg wrote. "Their friends are liberal, just as they are. They share the same values. Almost all of them think the same way on the big social issues of our time: abortion, gun control, feminism, gay rights, the environment, school prayer. After a while they start to believe that all civilized people think the same way they and their friends do. That's why they don't simply disagree with conservatives. They see them as morally deficient."

Bias topped *The New York Times* best-seller list in 2002. That, as it happened, would be a banner year for Roger Ailes and Fox News as well.

7

Is Ted Turner Nuts?

"I would like to see [Rupert Murdoch] selling newspapers on the corner where I started out. . . . That is what I think he deserves." —Ted Turner, *Time Warner Cable v. The City of New York and Bloomberg LP*, 1996

Jerry Levin was shaken when he put down the phone. "What the hell happened?" the Time Warner chief asked a fellow executive. "Rupert called and he went crazy on me."

The previous day, September 17, 1996, Levin had left his Rockefeller Center office in pouring rain and jogged across Sixth Avenue to the News Corp. headquarters. Ushered into Rupert Murdoch's office, Levin told his fellow mogul that after agonizing over the decision for weeks, he had finally decided that Time Warner Cable would carry MSNBC in lieu of Fox News Channel, which was set to launch in less than a month. Time Warner said that it did not have enough space on its systems to carry both of the fledgling news channels.

The decision was a huge blow to Murdoch. Time Warner was one of the nation's largest cable operators with 12 million subscribers, 1.1 million of them in New York City alone. Without access to the Time Warner system, Fox News would seldom be seen by advertisers, journalists, and the rest of Manhattan's media elite. That almost certainly meant reduced ad sales and publicity for a network that badly needed both. Worse, the deal would give MSNBC a total of 48 million subscribers in its first year, compared to just 17 million for Fox News. While Murdoch's cable news start-up faced daunting odds from the outset, the situation grew dire indeed without distribution on the Time Warner systems.

Murdoch initially seemed to accept Levin's news with equanimity. He nodded politely and said that he understood. But the next day he phoned the Time Warner boss in a rage, promising to give him hell. The decision to spurn Fox News, Murdoch thundered, was "an outrage." What followed was nearly a year of bitter warfare between two of the largest media companies in the world, replete with high stakes litigation, outrageous invective, and enormously entertaining publicity stunts. A headline in Murdoch's *New York Post* questioned Ted Turner's sanity. Turner, the liberal founder of CNN, called Murdoch a "scumbag" and likened him to Adolf Hitler. New York's best and brightest Republican politicians—including Mayor Rudolph Giuliani, Governor George Pataki, and Senator Alfonse D'Amato—enlisted in Murdoch's desperate mission. Even before it launched, the "fair and balanced" network was polarizing political debate. When the dust finally settled, the cable news wars had taken a fateful and possibly decisive turn.

After narrowly surviving some lean years in the early 1980s, CNN had for more than a decade enjoyed a virtual cable-news monopoly. But Turner's merger with Time Warner delivered an unpleasant consequence for CNN, one that meant its long reign as the only all-news network was coming to an end. CNN, which had about 68 million subscribers at the end of 1995, had long held some huge distribution advantages that virtually guaranteed its dominance in cable news. Operators such as Time Warner Cable and TCI held significant financial stakes in CNN as a result of their bailout of Turner's company in the late 1980s. The cable companies thus blocked any attempts by competitors to create rival services.

"I learned firsthand how the system works back in 1985," wrote former NBC News chief Larry Grossman. "We tried to launch a competing twenty-four-hour cable news service [at NBC] but were shut out the moment Turner sold an interest in his company to Time Warner, TCI, and other big cable franchise holders. . . . As a result, CNN held a monopoly in cable and the American people were denied access to any other national news channel." NBC was not alone. CBS also tried and failed to start an all-news cable network in the early 1990s. Murdoch complained in 1994 that he had wanted to start a news channel but the big cable operators "would not give me the time of day."

But all that changed with the Time Warner–TBS merger. As a condition of approving the deal, the Federal Trade Commission ordered Time Warner to open up its cable systems to rival programmers. In a consent decree, the media giant agreed to make at least one competing cable news channel available to at least half of its subscribers.

In the meantime, Murdoch was dangling huge sums of cash in front of operators who agreed to take Fox News. This was a reversal of the usual financial arrangement between programmers and cable systems. Traditionally, local cable companies pay a per-subscriber fee to programmers in exchange for a license to carry channels. The arrangement somewhat resembles how a movie exhibitor splits box-office revenue with a Hollywood studio. For example, cable operators in 1996 paid CNN an average of thirty-two cents per month per subscriber. If a system had one hundred thousand subscribers, the operator would send CNN a monthly check for $32,000. Multiply that amount to reflect the tens of millions of U.S. cable households, throw in advertising revenue, and you quickly begin to understand why CNN, MTV, ESPN, and other early cable networks developed a potent business model.

But Murdoch realized that most cable operators now needed a strong incentive to carry another news network. So he offered to pay a huge sum—at least $10 per subscriber and possibly as much as $20—to operators that carried Fox News Channel. While operators would still be required to pay subscriber fees once the network was up and running, the cash-for-subscriber offer amounted to an enormous advance. The bold move stunned insiders, because it represented a likely investment of hundreds of millions of dollars on behalf of a channel that didn't even exist. As Roger Ailes says, "Rupert is a man who can make a billion-dollar decision without blinking."

Murdoch soon found his first major taker: John Malone. The wily head of Tele-Communications Inc., at the time the country's largest cable operator, was a staunch conservative who, among other business traits, seemed violently allergic to any kind of tax. His political views naturally made him sympathetic to Murdoch's new right-leaning channel. But not surprisingly, it was money that clinched the deal. Perhaps the savviest operator the cable business ever produced, Malone found Fox News's cash-for-subscribers terms too good to pass up. On June 24, Fox News announced that it had secured a distribution agreement with TCI. The news release said that TCI would roll out Fox News to 90 percent of its subscribers, roughly 10 million customers, when the channel launched in the fall. In exchange, TCI would get an option to buy a 20 percent equity stake in Fox News.

The deal meant that Fox News was guaranteed an impressive number of subscribers when it launched. "As someone with great respect for cable operators," Roger Ailes said in a statement, "I am particularly pleased that our news channel has been accepted on its own merit." Of course, that was only part of the story. Murdoch paid TCI at least $100 million to carry the channel, which likely tipped the balance in Fox's favor.

With Malone in his pocket, Murdoch turned his attention to Time Warner Cable. But as it turned out, another company had the same idea in the summer of 1996. NBC, which had an agreement with Time Warner for America's Talking, now wanted the cable operator to renew the contract, with MSNBC taking the place of the since-defunct AT. It looked as though Levin would have to choose: Fox News or MSNBC.

At first it seemed that Murdoch had the upper hand. Ailes and Chase Carey, a top Murdoch lieutenant, negotiated for weeks with Time Warner's Fred Dressler, who hinted that a deal could be wrapped up as soon as the company closed its merger with Turner Broadcasting. "We had a deal in place," Ailes later said.

But GE would not be dismissed so easily. When Dressler informed NBC that America's Talking could not be used to launch the new joint venture with Microsoft, network executives threatened to sue. They pointed out that other cable operators had accepted the changeover, and a court would probably find it suspicious if the same company that owned CNN just happened to find a way to block MSNBC, especially after the FTC had just ordered competition in cable news. Besides, NBC was offering subscriber incentives comparable to those extended by Murdoch. Since Time Warner already had channel space reserved for America's Talking, it would not have to risk subscriber wrath by dumping another channel to carry MSNBC. Some of Malone's TCI systems had already drawn the ire of consumer watchdogs for ditching Lifetime in favor of Fox News. Finally, NBC had just purchased some new stations in key markets, and Time Warner would need the network's permission—so-called retransmission consent—to carry the signals of those outlets.

As the summer wore on, Time Warner briefly flirted with the idea of carrying both Fox News and MSNBC. Such an approach would hardly benefit CNN; on the other hand, the huge cash payments would probably hand Time Warner Cable its best year ever. At this point, Ted Turner, whose attention had been focused on the Time Warner merger, began to get involved. Turner was already worried about the potential impact of MSNBC and Fox News on CNN. "You don't have to be a rocket scientist to figure when you have Microsoft and General Electric on one side and News Corp. on the other coming at you, that that can have a major effect on your ratings and volume and profitability," he said.

Turner was incensed by the idea that Time Warner might carry not just one but two competitors to CNN. In addition to the damage it would wreak on his beloved news network, the move would delay the rollout of new Turner offerings such as Cartoon Network. "You're not taking the long-term view," Turner irritably told Levin. After lengthy debate, Levin ultimately agreed that taking both networks was probably a bad idea. Time Warner should choose one or the other.

Turner's real hope was that a decision on Fox or MSNBC could be deferred until one of the networks—or, better yet, both—melted away. Turner called Time Warner Cable chief Joe Collins and urged a go-slow approach. It might be possible to stick Fox on a few systems and MSNBC on a few others, so that neither network could mount an effective challenge to CNN. "My personal recommendation was that when [Collins] saw who was getting the most coverage on the other systems around the country between General Electric and News Corp., that he split the business between them," Turner said.

Levin and the other Time Warner executives felt that the FTC order did not afford them that kind of time. After conferring among themselves, they agreed that the deal with MSNBC made the most sense financially as well as practically. They could strike a deal with Murdoch later if they wanted. They called and broke the news to Turner, who later described himself as "disappointed." He wasn't the only one unhappy with the decision.

The night of October 1 was unseasonably warm in New York. Ice sculptures in the shape of Fox News Channel's new logo were melting quickly inside a tent on Forty-eighth Street, where Rupert Murdoch was hosting a party worthy of Orson Welles's fictional press baron

Charles Foster Kane. Former CBS co-anchor Connie Chung milled about in the throng of eight hundred, along with ABC News star Barbara Walters, Mayor Rudolph Giuliani, and Governor George Pataki.

The channel's launch was less than one week away. Senior staffers were grumbling about the 4 A.M. meeting Ailes had called for the next morning. But even that cloud failed to dampen the festive mood. Murdoch and Ailes received a special proclamation from Giuliani and Pataki. Giuliani declared that Fox News was of "incalculable value to the people of the city." The Republican mayor was referring to the fact that Fox would employ nearly one thousand local residents, although the fact that the network promised a rightward tilt likely sharpened Giuliani's eyes to its virtues.

Murdoch was still simmering over Jerry Levin's rejection of Fox News, but he and Ailes were determined to get even. They used the party as an opportunity to begin lobbying New York politicians. Fran Reiter, a top Giuliani aide, chatted a bit with Murdoch. Gossips buzzed about an intense conversation between Murdoch attorney Arthur Siskind and New York attorney general Dennis Vacco. "By the time of the party, it was pretty clear that we wanted any assistance that we could get," said Ailes, who had worked as an adviser on Giuliani's unsuccessful 1989 mayoral bid. "I said [to guests], 'Hey, how are you doing? We need your support.'"

Support was forthcoming. The very next day, the politicians began an extraordinary, and apparently coordinated, pressure campaign. Giuliani aides sent Time Warner a letter saying the city planned to carry Fox News on one of the five channels set aside for government and educational broadcasts (evidently to avoid the appearance of undue favoritism, city officials also sought to place Bloomberg Television, the small business news network controlled by billionaire Michael Bloomberg, on one of the other public channels). Meanwhile, both Senator D'Amato and Governor Pataki personally lobbed calls to Levin, urging that Time

Warner repeal the Fox News shutout. The governor told Levin that Murdoch himself had requested his help. Most dramatically, Vacco, acting on a suggestion from News Corp.'s Siskind, opened an antitrust investigation of Time Warner, and News Corp. sued its rival on antitrust grounds. Reiter threatened to revoke Time Warner's local cable franchise agreement with the city.

The GOP officials insisted that Murdoch's upstart network deserved protection because it would bring jobs to the city. But they conceded that politics also played a large role in their lobbying. Aides told *The New York Times* that "the officials resented what they saw as a liberal bias in the news media, so by helping Mr. Murdoch, they were protecting what they believed was the only media conglomerate with a conservative voice." Time Warner, they argued, was merely trying to protect its own bastion of liberal bias, CNN.

Time Warner officials were aghast by the campaign. Richard Aurelio, the veteran executive who headed up Time Warner's New York cable system, called the campaign "the most frightening exercise of political power that I have seen in my entire career." The Republican officials were trying "to endear themselves to somebody who has not only endorsed them in the past but continually supports them with biased coverage," he added. Consumer advocates accused the Giuliani administration of trying to blackmail Time Warner. Even executives from rival media companies entered the fray, noting dryly that many other programmers had been squeezed out of the New York cable market. Somehow, they noted, their distress had not been answered by an urgent phone call from the governor to the cable operator.

But for Murdoch, the political attack was merely prelude. News Corp. launched a full-scale media war, with Ted Turner as the principal target. When Turner's Atlanta Braves played in the World Series, Murdoch operatives hired a plane to circle Yankee Stadium carrying the sign: HEY, TED. BE BRAVE. DON'T CENSOR FOX NEWS CHANNEL. Murdoch's

New York Post took a different tack, with a headline that screamed IS TED TURNER NUTS? YOU DECIDE. A story inside averred that Turner was "veering dangerously toward insanity" and reminded readers that the CNN founder had taken lithium for depression.

When it came to Fox News, Murdoch was taking no chances. The *Post* also briefly dropped its program listings for CNN.

As the lawyers bickered, Ted Turner joked.

On the morning of October 18, Turner was deposed in a suit Time Warner filed against the City of New York. The mogul sat for hours answering questions in the Eighth Avenue offices of Cravath, Swaine & Moore, which represented Time Warner. Turner grew amused as Cravath lawyer Robert Joffe tangled with Martin Garbus, an attorney for Bloomberg Television. Bloomberg had joined the city's fight to put its network on one of the public channels and was also named a defendant in the suit. "This is like *Perry Mason,* for God's sake," Turner said, grinning. "Like the O.J. trial." At another point he compared the session to CNN's shout-a-thon *Crossfire,* in which liberal and conservative pundits square off. "Let's act civilized," he teased the attorneys.

But Turner grew serious when discussing his sworn archenemy. He called Murdoch a "scumbag" and "a pretty slimy character" and compared him to "the late Führer." According to Turner, Murdoch was a greed-driven monster who cynically used journalism as a tool in his world-domination scheme. "His journalistic credentials are a joke," Turner said. "He is a disgrace to journalism."

Turner viewed the Time Warner distribution battle as a typical Murdoch ploy. The CNN founder pointed out that rival cable networks frequently find themselves jockeying for distribution. Cable operators played networks against one another in search of the best deal. "Whoever didn't get the deal gets left out in the cold. That is just the way the game is played," Turner said. "That is what happened to Rupert."

The only difference this time, Turner argued, was that Murdoch had paid off powerful Republican politicians. He had made numerous large contributions to conservative causes over the years, including a $100,000 donation to the New York GOP, Turner said. One of the News Corp. divisions in 1995 had offered a $4.5 million book advance to then-House Speaker Newt Gingrich (the deal was later canceled after a scandal ensued). In the dispute over Fox News and Time Warner Cable, Turner claimed, powerful New York Republicans such as Pataki and Giuliani were simply carrying water for one of their party's most generous benefactors.

"I was just appalled that he bought the government of New York," Turner said, referring to Murdoch.

Asked his general views of Murdoch as a businessman, Turner replied, "I have no respect for him. I think he is a very dangerous person. . . . He uses the news media to advance his own personal position, mainly. He does so shamelessly. And he uses the power of the media to further his own personal wealth and power, rather than for the good of the communities which he is supposed to serve."

That sounds like the lament of a public advocate rather than a man whose aggressive deal-making had just made him vice chairman of the world's largest media company. There was reason to take Turner's bluster with a grain of salt; this was the same mogul, after all, who whined a couple of years earlier that Time Warner was "clitorizing" him. Yet it was natural that Turner would feel strong rivalry with the head of News Corp. Unlike most of the billionaire media moguls in the last decade of the twentieth century, Murdoch and Turner had made their fortunes largely in journalism. But Turner's antipathy was also fueled by something else. As a conservative-turned-liberal, he had grown to see his empire—and especially CNN—as more than just a business. Its founder believed that Turner Broadcasting was a positive force acting for the good of the community. True, sometimes Turner had been forced to push people around to make his businesses grow, but as he put it, "We play hard and we play fair." Had he used his networks as a bully pulpit to trash Murdoch? No—yet that was the sort of thing his competitor did without blinking. News Corp. was an enterprise devoted to winning, even at the cost of its soul. It all came from the corner office, and in Turner's view, the man ensconced there was selfish, unprincipled, indifferent to others—in a word, evil.

But at one point in his deposition, Turner made a telling slip. Publicly, he had championed the TBS merger with Time Warner, exulting that the combination would give him a chance to be a major player in global media. But now the mundane tasks of joining the companies—along with unforeseen complications, such as the FTC order to open up CNN to competition—were making him weary, if not remorseful. Asked for details of the merger, Turned blurted: "The whole thing has been kind of like a nightmare."

In early November, the judge in *Time Warner v. New York* handed down an opinion that ran for 106 pages. The verdict delivered another blow against Fox News.

U.S. District Court Judge Denise Cote found that the Giuliani administration had acted improperly in trying to convert the public channels for Fox News and Bloomberg. "The city's action violates long-standing First Amendment principles that are the foundation of our democracy," Cote found. "The city has engaged in a pattern of conduct with the purpose of compelling Time Warner to alter its constitutionally protected editorial decision not to carry Fox News." The judge issued a preliminary injunction barring the city from proceeding with its plan to carry Fox and Bloomberg.

The city appealed, but in July, the Second U.S. Circuit Court of Appeals upheld Judge Cote's injunction. In the meantime, the fight was spreading to other businesses. Time Warner filed suit in December after the Fox broadcast network threatened to pull its signals from cable systems in Tampa, Florida, and seven other markets. While News Corp. said the station dispute was not linked to the Fox News battle, Time Warner insisted that Murdoch was using strong-arm tactics to get his way in the Manhattan cable fight. Indeed, in newspaper ads, Fox ominously informed cable customers that they might not be able to see the NFL playoffs or Super Bowl if the Time Warner dispute was not resolved. Although the two sides agreed to a truce that avoided the football blackout, the upshot was clear. The Fox News battle was turning into a poisonous standoff that damaged both companies.

Fox appeared to be running out of options, but the company was not quite ready to surrender. Days after the appellate court ruled for Time Warner, Murdoch attended the media conference hosted every summer by investment banker Herbert Allen in Sun Valley, Idaho. Jerry Levin, Michael Eisner, and other moguls came to the meetings to relax and informally talk shop as reporters trolled for tips about possible upcoming deals. At one point Murdoch pulled Levin aside, and the two men began negotiating possible ways to solve the mess involving Fox News and Time Warner Cable.

Upon his return, Murdoch phoned Ailes. "We have a deal," he said.

It turned out that Murdoch craftily linked the Time Warner issue with another deal that was giving him problems. News Corp. was selling its troubled U.S. satellite operation, American Sky Broadcasting, to Primestar, a rival concern controlled by Time Warner and several other major cable operators. (Primestar was later sold to another satellite rival,

Hughes Electronics' DirecTV, which—irony of ironies—Murdoch bought in 2003 after years of attempts.) Murdoch and Levin both wanted the satellite talks to come off without a hitch.

So Murdoch tossed the Fox News issue into the overall deal for A Sky B. Levin agreed to guarantee Fox News 3 million subscribers by October 1997, plus another 5 million subscribers by 2001. In return, Time Warner would collect launch fees averaging $10 per subscriber, or roughly $80 million. Fox would also drop its antitrust suit against Time Warner, and Murdoch would be left with a nonvoting minority stake in the combined satellite operation. To clear space on the Manhattan system, the Giuliani administration agreed to forfeit one of its public channels in exchange for Time Warner's dropping its suit against the city.

Both sides tried to claim victory, but it was hard to dispute that Murdoch had gotten the better of Levin. The distribution deal by no means guaranteed Fox News's success, but at least the network had leveled the playing field. The best part was that Fox won immediate access to the Manhattan market. "New York is important," Ailes told reporters. "Opinion leaders live here, advertisers live here, the press thinks it's the only place in the world."

Over at Time Warner offices in Rock Center, many executives were scratching their heads. They argued that Levin could have extracted twice as much as he did in launch fees from Murdoch. And the city's "forfeiture" of a public channel was laughable, since the Giuliani administration had been trying to dump one of those channels for Fox News from the very outset. Time Warner had consistently emerged victorious in court, so why was the company settling with Murdoch on such generous terms? "We won every skirmish and then we lost the war," one executive said. "Everyone here is baffled."

Publicly, CNN tried to downplay Fox News's breakthrough. "We've faced competition before in our seventeen years, and we continue to be the world's leader in news and information," a spokesman said. "New York is just another part of our vast universe."

Behind the scenes, however, CNN had embarked on an ambitious plan to stave off the competition from Fox and MSNBC, a plan that would lead directly to the biggest scandal in the network's history.

8

"Valley of Death"

"It's been the most horrible nightmare I've ever lived through. . . . If committing suicide would help, I've even given that some consideration."
—Ted Turner on CNN's Tailwind fiasco

Tom Johnson was running late for a meeting at CNN Center in Atlanta. A keen sense of unease was beginning to creep up on him, but it was nothing compared to the remorse he and others at the network would soon feel. It was June 18, 1998.

"I just got off the phone with Henry Kissinger," the CNN News Group chairman told a roomful of producers and executives gathered for a tense conference call. Johnson was so upset, one attendee later recalled, that his knuckles were turning white as he spoke. "He told me this story makes him ashamed to be an American. He says it can't possibly be true."

The former Secretary of State, along with military officials and veterans groups, was incensed by "Valley of Death," an eighteen-minute investigative segment that CNN had broadcast eleven days earlier. The report asserted that in September 1970, during a secret mission or "black operation" code-named Tailwind, U.S. forces had used the nerve gas sarin in an effort to kill American defectors in Laos.

Everything about the allegation was explosive. A quarter century later, Americans remained highly conflicted about their role in the Vietnam War. It was difficult to square their overall view of the nation's uprightness with accounts of Vietnam-era atrocities such as the My Lai massacre and the secret bombings in Cambodia. Now CNN, the world's best-known news network, was accusing the U.S. military of Saddam Hussein–type tactics: using chemical weapons and then burying the story for nearly three decades. If true, the report exposed the hypocrisy of the U.S. government, which for years has chided Third World countries about their records regarding human rights and war crimes.

At first, CNN thought it had scored a major coup. "Valley of Death" was broadcast during the premiere of *NewsStand: CNN & Time,* a newsmagazine designed to flaunt the supposed corporate synergy between the network and Time Warner's far-flung magazine empire. The day after the "Valley of Death" broadcast, *Time* magazine hit the stands with an article based on the Tailwind report. Headlined DID THE U.S. DROP NERVE GAS? the *Time* story carried the bylines of April Oliver, a scrappy young CNN producer who had done much of the legwork for the segment, and Peter Arnett, the heroic correspondent from the 1991 Gulf War, who narrated the on-air report. While the ratings for the *NewsStand* debut were not particularly impressive, the Tailwind package seemed guaranteed to build buzz for the network. The night the report aired, CNN's special assignment unit, the group responsible for *NewsStand,* threw a party honoring Oliver. But within twelve hours there was trouble brewing in Atlanta.

Tailwind, the story that was going to help CNN regain its ratings momentum, was about to turn into the network's biggest nightmare, and the leadership failures that followed would deal CNN a major setback in its efforts to compete against Fox News and MSNBC.

When Ted Turner first laid eyes on Rick Kaplan, he brayed, "You're the biggest goddamned Jew I've ever seen!"

It was hardly an auspicious greeting for the man hired by Tom Johnson in August 1997 to revamp CNN's domestic channel, but there was little denying that Kaplan did cut an imposing figure. At six-foot-seven and 250 pounds, he was a broadcast news whiz who was jokingly called "Baby Huey" by his former colleagues at ABC News. Kaplan became legendary for his producing flair on *World News Tonight, PrimeTime Live,* and *Nightline.*

Kaplan had worked great magic at *World News Tonight,* taking a newscast that many regarded as an also-ran and turning it into a critics' favorite. He had a shrewd sense of narrative and visuals, and was particularly adept at "selling" a story—finding just the right angle that would have maximum impact for viewers. "He knew a good story and was merciless in his pursuit" of it, says news veteran Jeff Gralnick, Kaplan's friend and fellow producer on *World News Tonight.*

Kaplan's toughness won him the admiration of ABC News boss Roone Arledge. The Gralnick-Kaplan team "had a get-the-story-at-all-costs style, Darwinian by design, that drove out the less hardy," Arledge later wrote, adding, "If it hadn't been for ABC dropouts, how would Ted Turner ever have staffed his new CNN?"

Coworkers soon learned that Kaplan's giant frame was matched by an outsize self-regard. Kaplan had a short fuse and sometimes seemed to go out of his way to offend people; he was known to throw tantrums and dismiss opponents as "morons" or "liars." Once, in the midst of a violent argument at ABC News, Kaplan angrily attacked a fellow producer over an office intercom. "I wish you would die of cancer," Kaplan boomed over the loudspeaker, according to one witness. Even Sam Donaldson, the crusty *PrimeTime* cohost whom Kaplan idolized, complained to *TV Guide* about Kaplan's occasional "inability to get along with people the way you would hope." Kaplan, says one executive who knows him, is "kind of a frightened little boy in a very large body."

The brash producer sometimes pushed things too far on-screen as well as off. In November 1992, Kaplan's *PrimeTime* aired a report accusing the Food Lion grocery chain of unsanitary meat-handling practices. The company argued that, with the explicit approval of Kaplan and another producer, the two reporters who prepared the piece submitted bogus resumes to get jobs at two supermarkets, where they then shot hidden-camera footage. Food Lion sued Kaplan and ABC for fraud and trespass, eventually winning a judgment of $5.5 million (the suit was later settled out of court).

Kaplan also raised eyebrows within news circles for his remarkably close relationship with President Clinton and his wife. The trio became close in the late 1970s when Kaplan was a hotshot young producer on Walter Cronkite's *CBS Evening News* and Bill Clinton was the attorney general of Arkansas. During the 1980 presidential campaign, Kaplan hired Hillary Clinton to help prepare coverage. Years later, during the Clinton administration, Kaplan called to console Hillary after White House aide Vince Foster's suicide. Another time he invited Cuban dictator Fidel Castro to a dinner with President Clinton at the tony New York restaurant Café des Artistes (Castro declined). Most notoriously, the ABC producer spent a night in the Lincoln Bedroom in 1993, an event he afterward described in rapturous terms. "If you ever have a chance to sleep in the bedroom," he told a reporter, "do it." While Kaplan downplayed the friendship ("The fact is I don't talk to [President Clinton] very much at all," he told *Vanity Fair*), Donaldson and others within ABC News said that Kaplan was sensitive to criticism of the First Couple. He admitted that he urged colleagues to be "very careful" in describing Whitewater and other Clinton imbroglios as "scandals."

None of this deterred Tom Johnson, who began wooing Kaplan at least as far back as 1996, the same year that MSNBC and Fox went on the air. At the time, it was dawning on Johnson that CNN "was in for a major battle" with its new rivals. Johnson felt sure that Kaplan could help CNN produce hard-hitting magazine stories that, with the proper promotion, would get attention and grab ratings.

Kaplan was on a short list of candidates for the job of program director at CNN. He was in fine company; another person being considered was Jeff Zucker, then the wunderkind executive producer of NBC's *Today.* But Kaplan, convinced that his career had stalled at ABC, had bigger ideas. He was not interested in joining CNN unless it was prepared to spend much more money on programming. He also wanted to be named president of the entire domestic network. He wanted, in other words, the job title that Johnson already had.

Johnson agreed to step up newsroom spending, but the title was a problem. He took his dilemma to Turner, who had a ready solution.

"Make Kaplan president, I'll name you chairman," Turner told Johnson.

From the start, Kaplan set about shaking up CNN. In the early days, Turner's network was a boiler-room operation run by a skeleton crew of veterans and busloads of college kids. Salaries were low and stars were few. The emphasis was on bringing viewers the drama of breaking news. From that humble beginning, CNN had triumphed as the network to watch during the Gulf War of 1991. Now here was Kaplan, a veteran broadcaster who viewed CNN as a stodgy old cable network. It could stave off competition, he believed, only by upgrading itself to be *more like* its broadcast cousins. CNN needed better-known personalities, splashy programs, and more elaborate sets.

In December 1997, four months after joining the network (Roone Arledge called his departure "a terrific blow" to ABC News), Kaplan raided his old employer. He poached political analyst Jeff Greenfield and reporter Judd Rose from ABC News. Next he picked off Willow Bay, the coanchor of ABC's weekend version of *Good Morning, America.* The move especially surprised insiders because of Bay's marriage to Bob Iger, who was then the president of ABC.

The high-profile hires annoyed longtime CNN staffers, who believed that the newsroom budget was being devoured in a quest to glam up the network. Between 1989 and 1995, programming expenses for CNN and Headline News rose at a modest annual rate of roughly 10 percent, according to figures from Kagan World Media. In 1996, CNN and Headline News spent $120 million, a 22 percent increase over the previous year. The following year, when Kaplan was hired, costs rose another 18 percent. CNN's domestic network and Headline News spent nearly three times what Fox News spent on programming in 1997.

"Rick's [domestic channel] was given the highest priority . . . because of new competition from Fox and MSNBC," Johnson says. "That Rick got the largest percentage of the allocated extra budget dollars *did* annoy other channel heads at Headline News, CNN International, CNNfn, and other services."

CNN insiders believed the outlays would inevitably lead to belt-tightening elsewhere within the organization. "You can't do one of the network newsmagazines—which is what [Kaplan] was trying to do—on a cable news budget unless you're willing to strip a lot of other resources," says another executive.

What no one could deny, though, was that CNN's average ratings were eroding, and the competition from Fox and MSNBC threatened to make the problem much worse.

Kaplan had a solution: newsmagazines. If done correctly, these kinds of shows could get big ratings. Broadcasters recognized this and were increasingly relying on magazines to fill holes in their schedules. *60 Minutes* pioneered the format, but now NBC had *Dateline* and ABC had *20/20* and *PrimeTime Live.* All of these programs took on investigative pieces as well as celebrity interviews and lighter features. And all of them earned dependable ratings.

But the stories had to grab viewers' attention, make people sit up and take notice. Kaplan thought he found that kind of story for the premiere of *NewsStand*.

"I'm nervous about this story," Tom Johnson told a CNN colleague over lunch a few days before "Valley of Death's" June 7 airing. "I just . . . I don't think we've got it."

The colleague reminded Johnson that the network was an hour away from issuing a news release that would tease the content of the Sunday broadcast, promising juicy details of a military misadventure during Vietnam. If the chairman of the CNN News Group had any doubts about the story, he should by all means pull the plug immediately.

"No, no," Johnson replied. "Everybody's looked at it. Everybody says it's okay."

Indeed, Johnson believed in consensual decision-making, and a number of CNN producers and executives had signed off on the Tailwind report. "Valley of Death" passed muster with Pam Hill and Jim Connor, both experienced producers in CNN's investigative division. David Kohler, CNN's general counsel, had reviewed the segment and found no potential legal problems. Even Perry Smith, a retired Air Force major general paid by CNN to opine on military affairs, had given the report a thumbs-up when he first reviewed it.

Rick Kaplan was also confident of the report. The CNN/U.S. president spent the Saturday before the *NewsStand* premiere sitting in an editing bay, tweaking the segment with the producers. He told the crew he was sure the segment was a winner.

"Ultimately, I trusted the CNN team that they had it right—months of research, many interviews on and off camera, substantial vetting," Johnson says.

Hours before the broadcast, Johnson received a frantic phone call from General Smith. The CNN analyst said he'd asked around, and his military sources were convinced that the main thesis behind the Tailwind story wasn't true. CNN was making a big mistake, Smith said. The segment shouldn't run.

Johnson forwarded Smith to Kaplan, who in turn bounced him to Oliver and her coproducer, a gruff news veteran named Jack Smith (no relation to the general). The producers said their sourcing was solid. The story was good to go. Some at CNN believed that General Smith had merely been strong-armed by friends at the Pentagon who got wind of the report and knew it would make the military look terrible. The producers were not about to change or cancel the segment on account of a last-minute pressure campaign.

A few hours later, viewers around the nation saw the cohosts of *NewsStand,* Jeff Greenfield and Bernard Shaw, introduce "Valley of Death" on-camera with a startling accusation: "The United States military used lethal nerve gas during the Vietnam War."

The central theme was laid out starkly, with few qualifications. Essentially, the report said that a hit squad sponsored by the U.S. government had been armed with lethal gas in Laos. "The hunting and killing of American defectors was a high priority," Arnett, the segment's narrator and credited reporter, told viewers. The Tailwind operatives had "no rules [and] were pledged to secrecy," Arnett said. In CNN's telling, the mission had a cloak-and-dagger, *Third Man* air. There was little doubt about the network's point of view: the segment kept returning to a montage of black-and-white combat photos, backed by the Buffalo Springfield '60s war protest song "For What It's Worth."

Some of the report depended on unnamed sources, but it also featured an on-camera interview with retired Admiral Thomas Moorer, who served as chairman of the Joint Chiefs of Staff during Vietnam. Moorer offered some elliptical remarks that, depending on the interpretation, could be seen as confirming sarin usage during Tailwind. (Moorer had earlier earned a footnote in political history as head of the hawkish National Security Political Action Committee. In 1988, a group affiliated with NSPAC, Americans for Bush, produced the notorious Willie Horton commercial that tarred George H. W. Bush's presidential opponent, Massachusetts governor Michael Dukakis, as soft on crime.)

Reaction to the "Valley of Death" report came quickly, although it was not the sort that CNN expected.

"The early morning after Tailwind was broadcast," Johnson remembers, "I started receiving irate phone calls, faxes, and messages from [CNN] staffers who said they were being pounded with calls." Critics were accusing the network of airing a story that contained little concrete evidence of sarin usage and downplayed knowledgeable sources who insisted that Tailwind operatives were not targeting American defectors. Some conservatives were so angry they speculated that Ted Turner's liberal wife, Jane Fonda—whose visit with the Vietcong during the late 1960s earned her the nickname "Hanoi Jane"—was somehow behind the Tailwind broadcast.

Meanwhile, Moorer began to back away from the story, telling a wire service reporter he had only "heard rumors" about nerve gas being used. For their part, Oliver and her coproducer, Jack Smith, unequivocally stood by their entire report. But opposition continued to build.

On June 18, *The New York Times* published a scathing 1,141-word op-ed by former Green Beret John L. Plaster, who had served as a source months earlier when Oliver was conducting more general research of special-operation maneuvers in Vietnam. "If you stare too hard into the shadows," Plaster began, "sometimes you don't see what is really there, only what you imagine ought to be there." Plaster blasted Oliver by name for ignoring doubts raised by him and other veterans prior to the Tailwind broadcast. He ended by repeating a longstanding gripe of military veterans: Americans' supposed ingratitude for U.S. troops' sacrifice during Vietnam. "If CNN and *Time* are any measure," he concluded, "there seems little gratitude today either."

Johnson, now wracked by doubts, grew desperate. He cracked open his formidable Rolodex and did some reporting of his own. He says that, in addition to Kissinger, he called Colin Powell, former chairman of the Joint Chiefs of Staff, and ex-CIA director Richard Helms.

"My calls to [them] were to try to confirm our report—to see if they had any additional information about a black operation in Laos to substantiate the report," Johnson says. "General Powell strongly believed [CNN's report] was in error. Dick Helms, an old friend, had no recollection of such a mission. Dr. Kissinger, also an old friend, was especially upset because he felt that our producers had tried to tie the mission somehow to him and to the [National Security Council]. The more I heard from men I had known since my own White House years, the more uncomfortable I felt about the report," Johnson says.

During the June 18 teleconference, when Johnson revealed his conversation with Kissinger, Kaplan told other CNN executives, "This is not a journalism problem. It is a PR problem."

Actually, Tailwind was problematic as both journalism and PR. CNN had tried to prove a thesis that was all but unprovable. The mission in question took place nearly three decades earlier. Recollections by sources were predictably hazy and often contradictory. Because Tailwind was a secret mission, there was no paper trail. And because anything having to do with Vietnam was so highly politicized, everyone involved—reporters, sources, executives—had complicated motives that were themselves worthy of investigation. Seen from that light, the Tailwind report revealed a certain naive optimism on CNN's part: Chasing Tailwind was akin to promising to get to the bottom of President Kennedy's assassination. That CNN—which was known for breaking news, not groundbreaking investigations—chose such a story to launch a high-profile new series is striking and suggests the intense pressure the network was under to boost ratings.

Tailwind also suffered from horrible timing. American journalism seemed to be suffering from a credibility crisis in 1998. The month before "Valley of Death" aired, the *New Republic* fired Stephen Glass, a young writer who admitted to fabricating numerous stories and sources. Around the same time, the *Cincinnati Enquirer* published a lengthy exposé of banana purveyor Chiquita; the newspaper apologized and retracted the story in late June after one of the reporters was said to have stolen private voice mails from the company. Media critics did not treat all this as mere coincidence; for many reporters, three recent instances of any phenomenon is evidence of a bona fide trend. Tailwind seemed to fit a pattern of journalistic misadventure.

Johnson worried that if the network didn't address the issue head-on, the stench of a cover-up would settle over CNN Center. He proposed to Ted Turner that the network hire Floyd Abrams, a First Amendment attorney beloved by journalists for his work on the Pentagon Papers case in the early 1970s, to investigate the "Valley of Death" broadcast. Turner agreed.

As coinvestigator, CNN chose an unlikely candidate: the network's general counsel, David Kohler, who had vetted "Valley of Death" prebroadcast and okayed its airing. Moreover, in a confidential memo to Johnson on June 16, Kohler had written that he could not "argue the underlying story is correct; we may never know that given the nature of the operation"—an insight that might have proven more helpful before rather than after the broadcast.

Over the next two weeks, Abrams and Kohler interviewed Oliver and Smith, along with a number of their sources. They also talked to critics of the program and reviewed some research gathered by Kroll Associates, a private investigation firm with many corporate clients.

Abrams and Kohler delivered their fifty-four-page report to CNN on July 2. Turner was originally against making the contents public, but Johnson persuaded him that the network had to come clean. The entire document soon found its way onto CNN's popular Web site.

The attorneys began by praising the Tailwind report as "rooted in extensive research" and a reflection of "the honestly held conclusions of CNN's journalists." The rest of their appraisal was harsh. Abrams and Kohler vigorously attacked the Tailwind sourcing. Moorer's statements were quoted at length and ultimately deemed to be "attenuated and inconclusive." Another source, former Lieutenant Robert Van Buskirk, who had recalled killing Caucasians during the Tailwind operation, was found unreliable partly because of his medical history, including a past "nervous disorder." The attorneys said that "Valley of Death" generally ignored other sources who disputed the segment's central thesis.

The bottom line was that the Tailwind segment was "insupportable," the lawyers wrote. "CNN should retract the story and apologize."

Johnson wasted no time doing exactly that. On July 2, CNN ran a videotape of Johnson reading a prepared statement. "We acknowledge serious faults in the use of sources who provided *NewsStand* with the original reports and therefore retract the Tailwind story," he said. "CNN's system of journalistic checks and balances, which has served CNN exceptionally well in the past, failed in this case. The fault lies with the editors, producers and reporters and executives responsible for the report, the program, and its contents." He added that the network was "taking vigorous steps" to avoid such mistakes in the future.

Then the bloodletting began. Johnson fired Smith—who, ironically, had given Kaplan one of his first broadcasting jobs—and Oliver, who says she was escorted out of CNN's Washington bureau by a security guard. Both were livid at their treatment.

"Tom Johnson, who is not a brave man under the best of circumstances, absolutely panicked," Oliver says. Retracting the report and firing the producers "was a purposeful strategy by CNN's management to get out from under." She charges that CNN made a "business decision" to retract Tailwind. "The frigging Pentagon picked up the phone and told CNN, 'We have Fox, we have MSNBC, we don't need you anymore, CNN.' CNN saw their revenue stream from wartime access potentially being pulled out from under [them]."

Johnson also wanted to fire Peter Arnett. He felt the fabled correspondent had done virtually nothing to ascertain the accuracy of the report. But Ted Turner intervened. The CNN founder "asked that we let Peter work out his contract because of his bravery and exclusive coverage during the Gulf War," Johnson says. Even so, Arnett—whom CNN had brandished for years as its biggest star correspondent—virtually disappeared from the airwaves for months as the network let his contract expire.

Johnson called a series of soul-searching meetings with CNN staffers. "It felt like we were in this giant group therapy," says Greta Van Susteren, a CNN host and legal analyst who was not involved in preparing the Tailwind segment. "I'll never forget one day. I was supposed to be on the air at 12:30 Eastern with my show, and we were all to report at noon to the conference room. And we had this network-wide group meeting about Tailwind. It was . . . people baring their souls, saying, 'This is the worst thing that ever happened.' Everyone sort of got into this very mawkish [tone]. We were going around the room. It was so weird. . . . The way it was handled, there was so much 'mea culpa, mea culpa.' "

Finally, Johnson offered his own resignation to Turner and the Time Warner board.

"They were very concerned about the mistake, the hit we took on our credibility," Johnson says. "I offered to resign because I was responsible for the mistake. I permitted a report to be broadcast which was unsubstantiated—and now I do not believe there is sufficient evidence that it is true." But neither Turner, who still had warm feelings for his longtime lieutenant, nor the board would accept Johnson's offer. He had survived—for the moment.

Kaplan considered resigning but ultimately decided against it. While he called the retraction "totally devastating," he soon set about trying to find other headline-grabbing stories for *NewsStand.* "We'll get through this," he told the *Atlanta Journal-Constitution.*

As the Tailwind affair played out, Kaplan was fighting on another front at CNN. This time the battle spilled over on-camera.

Lou Dobbs was one of the few people at CNN who had an ego as colossal as Kaplan's. Both were large men with larger-than-life personalities, but in other ways they were natural opposites. Dobbs, for instance, was a pro-business Republican who was deeply uncomfortable with Kaplan's wide-ranging connections in the Democratic Party. The influential *Moneyline* anchor had initially supported the idea of hiring Kaplan for the relatively circumscribed job of program director, but he was irked when Kaplan got the nod as president. "Rick is in my opinion an extraordinarily talented and accomplished executive producer," Dobbs says, "but he had absolutely no executive experience whatsoever."

What miffed Dobbs even more was the *NewsStand* deal cooked up with the Time Warner magazines. While *NewsStand* was a corporate undertaking, Dobbs viewed the series primarily as a Kaplan project. One of the *NewsStand* shows would be linked with *Fortune,* Time Warner's venerable business magazine, and it appeared that Dobbs would have no control over its content. "I was responsible for all business programming," says Dobbs, who in addition to his on-air duties also served as president of CNNfn, Turner's upstart financial news network. "I think [the *Fortune* venture was] a little bit of an intrusion, if you will, into my bailiwick," Dobbs says.

Dobbs complained to Johnson, who gently advised him to back off and let Kaplan do his job. "Tom said, 'We'll make this work. Appreciate you doing this,'" Dobbs says. "So I was a good soldier."

But resentments lingered. On May 20, 1999, nearly a year after the Tailwind uproar, Dobbs was in the middle of his *Moneyline* broadcast when Kaplan, sitting in the control room, ordered the crew to cut away to Littleton, Colorado. President Clinton was making an appearance there in the wake of the Columbine school shootings. Earlier in the program, *Moneyline* featured some coverage of Clinton's appearance, and Dobbs thought that was enough. "My response was, 'We've done Littleton. Relax. It's all taken care of,'" Dobbs says. "I assumed [Kaplan] hadn't seen the first part of the show."

Then in his earpiece Dobbs heard "a loud noise . . . which was Rick apparently exploding, insisting that we go back" to Clinton.

"My first thought was to tell him to go straight to hell," Dobbs says. Instead, the veteran anchor stared into the camera and curtly told viewers: "CNN president Rick Kaplan wants us to return to Littleton."

After the controller switched to President Clinton, the crew told Dobbs that Kaplan wanted to speak with him by phone right away. Dobbs said he would call in when he got the chance. He never did. "I didn't get the opportunity," he says. Dobbs thought he was justified in making it clear to viewers who made the Littleton decision. "I had never in my life received an order from a president of this company or anyone else on what to do with my broadcast," he says. "This was the first time in history."

But for CNN management, already besieged by the Tailwind affair, Dobbs's fit of pique was not amusing. "Lou was wrong, and he let his emotions spill over to CNN's air," Johnson says.

Two weeks later, Dobbs stunned CNN's New York bureau staff at 5 Penn Plaza in New York by announcing he was leaving the network after nearly twenty years. The anchor had threatened to walk out before, most memorably in 1990 when he was passed over as CNN president in favor of Tom Johnson. Back then, Ted Turner had prevailed upon him to stay. This time, though, Dobbs and his employers seemed to have had their fill of each other.

Dobbs was a major investor in a new Web site devoted to space exploration. The press made fun of the project (a headline in the *New York Observer* asked, LOU DOBBS: SPACE COWBOY OR SPACE CADET?). But Time Warner became unhappy with his increasing involvement with Space.com, and the Kaplan dispute had not helped.

"Ted and I told Lou he could not be a major equity participant and leader of Space.com and head of CNN business news, CNNfn, and anchor of *Moneyline,*" Johnson says. "It was an impossible conflict."

Asked later why he left, Dobbs could not resist taking another jab at Kaplan. "I left because I was tired of what I perceived to be the liberal side of the network and the cozy relationship between Mr. Kaplan and Clinton," he says half-jokingly.

In any event, Dobbs's departure gave CNN another ill-timed hit to its pocketbook. Under his tenure, *Moneyline* was the top-rated business program on cable and probably CNN's most profitable show. During the second quarter of 1999, the program averaged 366,000 households. For the same period a year later—with Kaplan hire Willow Bay and longtime financial journalist Stuart Varney as coanchors—*Moneyline*'s ratings plunged 38 percent.

Tailwind's blowback dogged CNN for years. The scandal suggested that CNN, which had built its name on spot news reporting, was unable to deliver the kind of in-depth magazine journalism that CBS News knocked off each week on *60 Minutes.* Time Warner was dealt a humiliating blow in its efforts to foster synergy between its magazine division and CNN. Most important, the harsh reaction to "Valley of Death" marred CNN's vaunted reputation for accuracy and fairness, and deepened an impression among many viewers that the network was biased against the government, particularly the military. That played right into the hands of Fox News, which built a marketing slogan around "fair and balanced" coverage.

Oliver sued CNN over her firing, charging that the network defamed her with the Abrams-Kohler report and subsequent public statements. Time Warner, apparently not eager to have Ted Turner and other executives deposed in a bitter legal fight, settled with her in the spring of 2000. One knowledgeable source estimates that the company paid Oliver $3 million. Her attorney, Roger Simmons, would only go on record to say that his client won "a nice settlement." According to Oliver, Simmons took a standard contingency fee of 30 percent. (Attorneys for CNN, April Oliver, and Jack Smith say that those figures are "substantially inaccurate" but declines to comment further).

Simmons also represented Oliver's coproducer, Jack Smith, in his suit against CNN. He and the company settled in the spring of 2002 for a payout estimated in the $1 million range.

Six Tailwind sources filed their own lawsuits. One was Robert Van Buskirk, the former lieutenant who had remembered killing Caucasians during the raid. He sued Time Warner and CNN in June 1999, arguing that the network had defamed him both in the original Tailwind broadcast and also in the Abrams-Kohler report and subsequent on-air statements, which had alluded to his "nervous disorder" in dismissing his credibility. In March 2002, the Ninth Circuit U.S. Appeals Court rejected Van Buskirk's argument that the producers defamed him, but determined that Abrams and Kohler may have. "CNN's statements [in the Abrams-Kohler report] could have given the impression that Van Buskirk was mentally ill," Judge Myron Bright wrote in his opinion. "The statements . . . may have created a false impression that Van Buskirk's use of (or need for) medication was the cause of CNN's erroneous story on Operation Tailwind." The judge remanded the case to the district court for further review.

The opinion cast doubt on the very report that Johnson had relied on in trying to correct what he viewed as the worst mistake of his career.

Johnson blamed himself for the Tailwind debacle, saying that he should have paid more credence to the doubts raised by General Smith. But Johnson's real mistake, it seems, was in not listening to himself. He had doubts about Tailwind but chose not to act on them. He had counted the votes beforehand, and they favored airing the segment.

"I trusted my staff to get it right. We didn't," Johnson says. "I will regret this mistake all the days of my personal and professional life."

9

Fake Brick and Aunt Fanny

"This is a hell of a moment in the history of NBC News. . . . We have created something that will be constantly changing." —Andy Lack, upon MSNBC's July 1996 launch

Phil Griffin was sitting in the MSNBC control room one evening in September 1996 when the phone rang. The two-month-old network was in the middle of airing *Internight,* a prime-time magazine/talk show executive produced by Griffin, a former *NBC Nightly News* producer. That night's show was devoted entirely to the state of the Catholic Church in America. A former priest talked about his decision to leave the clergy, and religion experts pondered whether modernizing reforms might be necessary for the Church to attract more young Americans.

The control-room caller did not like what he saw. "What are you doing?" NBC News chief Andy Lack demanded of Griffin. "Are you out of your mind? Nobody is going to watch this. Was this Brokaw's idea? I hope it was, because I certainly hope *you* wouldn't do this. I'd rather watch color bars."

Griffin knew his boss had a point. *NBC Nightly News* anchor Tom Brokaw, who served as one of *Internight*'s rotating hosts, had indeed lobbied to do a show about Catholicism. While religion could make a compelling topic, this particular program had no particular news hook or angle that might intrigue casual viewers. That pointed to a larger issue with *Internight,* one of MSNBC's signature shows: Viewers never knew what to expect. Just the night before, the program had featured lighthearted chats with baseball manager Tommy Lasorda and sitcom actor Phil Hartman. Now it was spending an entire hour academically debating the future of one of the world's major religions.

Griffin quickly resolved that the Church show would never enter MSNBC's repeat roster. But the incident offered a harbinger of problems that would soon beset the network jointly owned by NBC and Microsoft. Unlike Fox News, MSNBC could never quite figure out what it wanted to be. Was it a hip tech channel? A breaking news service? A documentary channel? A talk network? Competitors had initially feared that, backed by the extensive resources of NBC News, the network would end up dominating the cable news landscape. MSNBC instead spent the first seven years of its existence careering among various strategies, never settling on one that gave the network a distinct identity.

The story of how that happened offers a dramatic counterpoint to the rise of Fox News, proving that even large, committed companies with deep news experience can lose their way in the odd world of cable television.

In some respects, Andy Lack seemed the perfect person to lead a new twenty-four-hour cable news network. For starters, he was fully on board with GE's demand that NBC News produce ever greater revenue and profits.

"GE, and Jack [Welch] in particular, was pressing NBC, all of us in our respective areas, for growth," Lack says. "And it was pretty clear to us at NBC News that the most obvious place to grow your business was to get into the news business twenty-four hours a day instead of basically six or seven hours a day, which is where we were."

Equally important, Lack was regarded as a visionary for his impressive rescue of NBC News. The division had gone through some terrible years prior to Lack's arrival in 1993. His immediate predecessor was Michael Gartner, who had presided over one of the worst scandals in broadcast news history. In a story about the safety of certain GM trucks, the newsmagazine *Dateline* included a fifty-seven-second video that purported to show a vehicle exploding on impact. GM investigators later proved that NBC had rigged the crash with miniature explosives.

Even without the *Dateline* fiasco, NBC News—once the home of fabled newscasters Chet Huntley and David Brinkley—was by the early 1990s a deeply demoralized place, buffeted by years of downsizing and high-profile defections. Since Gartner took over in 1988, the company cut costs by closing more than ten of its foreign bureaus and lost such well-known correspondents as Connie Chung. Most depressing were the ratings. *Nightly News* had been mired in third place for so long that Brokaw, in a bit of gallows humor, called it "the network version of *Home Alone.*"

NBC chief Bob Wright looked to Lack as a leader who would finally restore NBC News to its erstwhile glory. A former ad man, Lack had spent seventeen years as a controversial producer at CBS News. His crowning achievement was *West 57th,* a short-lived but influential newsmagazine with a jazzy score, jumpy editing, and lively young hosts. *West 57th* bothered many of the purists at CBS—always the most staid of network news divisions—but soon other newsmagazines copied its style. Lack first came to Wright's attention when Brokaw sought to lure him over to NBC as executive producer of *Nightly News.*

Ensconced at Rock Center, Lack brought a fresh take to news coverage. He downplayed foreign and political stories, favoring instead pieces on health, science, and pop culture. "I point to the areas of health and science because they've always been the unglamorous stocks in the newsroom," he told authors Leonard Downie Jr. and Robert G. Kaiser.

"But in fact they are the real news in people's lives." He also flooded NBC with high-rated coverage of the O. J. Simpson murder trial.

Under Lack's watch, NBC shows such as *Today, Dateline,* and *Nightly News* soared in the ratings, eventually dominating their time slots. *Today,* in one of its most successful moves, inaugurated a street-level studio in Rockefeller Center, a signature that was soon imitated by competitors, including CNN. NBC News became enormously profitable, some years raking in more than $300 million in profits.

Lack "gave NBC News an entirely new identity," says anchor Brian Williams. "He arrived when the place was on its knees, and he gave that place identity and he made them feel good about themselves."

Lack became a larger-than-life fixture within the network. A serious antiques collector and incorrigible Anglophile, he was tall, dazzling, charismatic, and—thanks in no small part to his unit's bolstered balance sheet—much beloved at the GE headquarters in Fairfield, Connecticut. GE boss Jack Welch, who palled around with the likes of President Clinton and Jerry Seinfeld, called the NBC News chief one of the most fascinating people he had ever met. Even his background was rich with drama: When he was six, his gambler father—"a charming guy, a Damon Runyon figure," in Lack's phrase—left the family and was some months later shot to death during a card game. (As a teenager, Lack learned details of the murder by reading old clippings in the morgue of the *New York Daily News.*) But even those who knew nothing about his background found the NBC News chief a memorable presence, especially by the button-down standards of GE. The executive had a deep, booming voice that he often used to command attention; his thinning brown hair usually looked as if it needed combing. "He was larger than life, he would overwhelm a room," Brian Williams says of Lack.

Even after he became an executive, Lack kept paying attention to the details of production, sometimes to the dismay of his staff. Seated in his office, he would frequently glance over a visitor's shoulder at a monitor tuned to MSNBC or an NBC News broadcast. When he noticed something he did not like—a boring guest, say, or graphics that were hard to read—he immediately called the control room to harangue the staff. "Do you need me to come and produce this myself?" he would say. "My Aunt Fanny could produce a better show."

Humility was not Lack's long suit. During an interview with *The New York Times,* he alluded to the success of NBC News during his tenure, boasting, "I am America's news leader." The remark became notorious within the business. Some wags at Fox News memorialized the quote by sending media reporters a composite photo of Lack's head superimposed on Napoleon's body, one hand thrust inside his waistcoat and another resting purposefully on a globe.

Shortly before MSNBC was unveiled, Andy Lack met Brian Williams for dinner in New York. Williams, a rising star at NBC News, already looked destined to take over Tom Brokaw's anchor desk. As the White House correspondent and weekend anchor, Williams in many ways resembled Brokaw's kid brother: authoritative, photogenic, unflappable, quick-witted, and—although he was in fact from New Jersey—seemingly midwestern in accent and demeanor. The network felt so confident in Williams that when executives were trying to woo him away from his news job at WCBS in New York, Brokaw himself met with the candidate and confided that he was looking for a successor on *NBC Nightly News.*

Brokaw was not likely to retire for years, however, and Lack had big plans about what to do in the meantime with his would-be successor. At dinner he excitedly told Williams that NBC was about to leap into the cable news business with Microsoft. Williams would be pulled off the

White House beat and made the lead anchor and managing editor of a prime-time newscast on the new network. This would be a different kind of news hour, Lack said. The audience would be busy working parents who had missed *Today* and *Nightly News.* Williams could show these viewers what had happened earlier that day, as well as the stories that would make headlines in tomorrow's papers. The 9 P.M. slot on MSNBC would be the perfect proving ground for the future *Nightly News* anchor.

Williams was intrigued, but he wondered how NBC would fill the rest of the hours on an all-news network. Lack had given this much thought. He had a vision of "ongoing conversation": When news was not happening, a regular crew of talking heads would engage in literate banter amid a hip-looking studio decked out in fake brick and halogen lights. The network would be aimed at the young adults who were migrating to the Internet, with a backdrop reminiscent of one of the Seattle coffee bars that were growing popular among the Web-savvy crowd. MSNBC would be like Roger Ailes's America's Talking channel, shot inside a Starbucks outlet. "People are going to be on television, having coffee," Lack said.

As a traditional newsman, Williams was nonplussed. "Well, that's really something," he thought. "We're gonna be a coffee channel."

Williams was hardly the only one with doubts. Many NBC staffers hated the name chosen for the new network. "MSNBC" was a mouthful. Some half-jokingly pointed out that the letters MS made viewers think not of Microsoft but rather multiple sclerosis. Moreover, while Lack had promised that MSNBC would fully tap the resources of NBC News, many of the network's top stars were not enthusiastic about appearing on an upstart cable network. In addition to Brokaw, the rotating hosts of *Internight* included Bob Costas, Katie Couric, Bryant Gumbel, and Bill Moyers.

Griffin had the unenviable job of trying to persuade these luminaries to do the show regularly. "None of them wanted to do it," he says. Once, when Brokaw got a half-hour interview with basketball legend Michael Jordan, the producers out of desperation stretched the chat to a full hour "because I knew I wouldn't get Brokaw for another couple of weeks," Griffin says. *Internight* was originally supposed to air live at 8 P.M., but given their crowded schedules, the hosts soon began insisting that the show be taped in advance. After a while, even that became a burden. "It was, 'Hey, could you help me out, Phil? Don't put me on for a couple of weeks,'" Griffin says. The producers increasingly relied on backup hosts such as John Gibson (who later migrated to Fox News) and John Siegenthaler.

As it turned out, cable viewers weren't necessarily excited by the prospect of Couric and Brokaw anyway. The medium really demanded its own stars, not personalities borrowed secondhand from broadcast. "Andy Lack went into this thinking that the sensibility he learned in broadcast—and he had a very good gut, by the way, in broadcast—would immediately translate into cable and this new world," Griffin says. But "the cable news audience doesn't want that group of people. They can get them on the [broadcast] network."

Within days of launching in the summer of 1996, MSNBC distinguished itself with coverage of TWA Flight 800, which had crashed mysteriously in the Atlantic shortly after its New York takeoff. Exploiting the resources of NBC News, the channel had video of the disaster scene before any other network, including CNN.

But like CNN, the network soon faced the problem of what to do when there was no breaking news. Lack's bold, tech-oriented vision was ambitious, trendy, and enormously risky. Technology gurus in the mid-1990s were predicting that the Internet was about to meld with television in a phenomenon known as convergence. It was believed that within a few years a majority of Internet users would have access to high-speed network connections. Viewers would be able to download high-quality video on their computers, and they would surf the Net on their TVs. Media soothsayers spoke of an "information superhighway." The Web and television should not be looked at as two discrete entities, Lack and others believed, but rather as related media that would reach their greatest potential in tandem. NBC was making a huge bet that by exploiting convergence early, it would prevail in the news wars.

MSNBC's slogan, repeated in endless promos, was "It's time to get connected." Some, though not all, of the initial programming emphasized that theme. In addition to *Internight*—an intentional pun on "Internet," although in practice the show rarely had anything to do with technology—there was *The Site,* a one-hour program at 10 P.M. aimed squarely at young people who were beginning to flock to the Internet. The idea was to explain technology in ways that laypeople could understand. In addition to interviewing Silicon Valley executives and software designers, host Soledad O'Brien was shown chatting with a hip animated character named Dev Null whose job was to elaborate on technical concepts for viewers.

Like many new cable networks, MSNBC did not receive ratings when it first launched. Staffers were therefore shocked in February 1997 when the first Nielsen data arrived. The numbers showed that MSNBC was averaging 27,000 households in prime time—better than the 16,000 for Fox News but a mere fraction of the 522,000 for CNN.

"We thought hundreds and hundreds of thousands of people, if not millions, were watching us," Griffin says. "We had no idea. We were a little blown away that nobody was watching. I mean, we just didn't know the cable news world."

Luckily, the network did not have to wait long for another huge breaking story. In August 1997, Princess Diana was killed in a car crash in Paris, and her elaborate funeral—along with the ongoing investigation surrounding the accident—spiked cable news viewing for weeks afterward. MSNBC offered nonstop coverage of the tragedy that preempted much of the regular programming. When the Princess Diana coverage finally ebbed, some shows did not return to the lineup, including *The Site.*

As MSNBC's programming floundered, the relationship between its two corporate partners soured.

The deal had no sooner wrapped than NBC executives were congratulating themselves for getting the better of their counterparts at Microsoft. Essentially the agreement minimized risk for the network while offloading as many costs as possible onto the software maker. GE could at least theoretically spread the programming costs of MSNBC across multiple networks, including NBC and CNBC. Microsoft had to share the channel's start-up costs, launch and operate the accompanying Web site, and pay NBC an annual license fee of $20 million to boot.

Microsoft chief Bill Gates, who had held off signing the deal with GE's Jack Welch until minutes before their December 1995 press conference, began to resent the partnership. "As he learned about the deal . . . and how much more advantageous it was financially to NBC than to Microsoft, he began to hate it," says one former NBC executive. Gates became increasingly vocal about his unhappiness during meetings of MSNBC's joint board, which included GE's Jack Welch. "Jack would get a real kick out of the fact of how pissed off Bill was," the former NBC executive says. "We'd go to a board meeting, and Bill would be pissed off at the financials."

"We felt that the structure of the contract was too favorable to NBC as things worked out," explains former Microsoft executive Peter Neupert.

Gates became especially angry when he realized that MSNBC's acclaimed Web site—run by Internet visionary Merrill Brown—was struggling financially, even as distribution for the cable channel grew rapidly despite its low ratings.

Microsoft objected when NBC proposed airing *The News with Brian Williams* on CNBC as well as MSNBC. The network argued that the dual broadcasts would increase awareness of the newscast, but Microsoft countered that the move would dilute the MSNBC brand. NBC eventually overrode Microsoft's complaints and began airing *The News* on CNBC.

Microsoft also pressed NBC to get its local affiliates more involved with MSNBC, but broadcast stations were not eager to help promote a new cable network. Many had their own news operations and Web sites, and they worried that they would be upstaged by the new joint venture. "We had outlined some money to . . . make it easier to promote the cable channel locally," Neupert says. "And it wasn't clear that all that was going to work out like we'd hoped."

NBC staffers rolled their eyes at some of Microsoft's promotional demands. Producers at *NBC Nightly News,* for instance, are ordered every day to come up with the "MS tease," a story that will conclude with the anchor telling viewers to log on to MSNBC for more information. Microsoft has seen to it that NBC takes the promotion seriously. "If you're gonna kill it from that night's broadcast, you had better have good reason," says one top news staffer.

Bob Wright says the various tensions at times made Microsoft a "difficult" partner. The feeling at Microsoft was mutual. "I think some of what Bob says is fair," Neupert says, but "I could argue that NBC was a difficult partner. I think people that have strong brands and strong personalities and strong points of view and multiple interests by definition are difficult partners."

Soon MSNBC was regarded at the Microsoft campus as one of the company's few strategic mistakes. Steve Ballmer, who became CEO of Microsoft in January 2000, was a frequent internal critic of the cable network, at times expressing regret about MSNBC's very existence. "If we were starting [MSNBC] now, as good an operation as it is, I don't think we would have started it," Ballmer told reporters in 2001.

As Fox News began to surge in the ratings, Lack hit upon another programming concept: nostalgia.

One of the few initial MSNBC shows that drew a decent audience was *Time & Again,* a 7 P.M. clip show hosted by Jane Pauley. The program raided the NBC archives, which contained more than eight hundred thousand videotapes, for footage of old news events such as Ted Kennedy's Chappaquiddick accident, a Tom Snyder interview with John Lennon, or the wedding of Prince Charles and Princess Diana. Pauley then added taped introductions and news quizzes designed to test viewers' memories of the era in question.

"Our video time capsule is the kind of programming concept that truthfully deserves its own twenty-four-hour network," Lack bragged to reporters when MSNBC launched in July 1996.

It was hardly groundbreaking programming, but *Time & Again* offered two enormous benefits for MSNBC: It was very cheap to produce, and it could be repeated endlessly. Some NBC executives pointed out to Lack that other cable networks had seen ratings growth with similar retrospective programs, notably A&E's *Biography* and VH1's *Behind the Music.* So Lack tried another clip program, a celebrity profile show called *Headliners & Legends,* hosted by *Today*'s Matt Lauer.

Some staffers felt that MSNBC was straying from hard news coverage and drifting into soft features. "If you played the guitar in one *Par-*

tridge Family episode, there's a half-hour show about you in the MSNBC archives," Brian Williams jokes.

Other insiders felt the move toward documentaries was a logical, if not exactly desirable, evolution. Despite his years as a news producer, Lack had little experience with live television and—prior to MSNBC, at least—no experience at all with cable. "Andy [moved] back to what he knew best, which was documentaries and tape," Griffin says. "He came out of *West 57th,* CBS, and *60 Minutes,* and that kind of thing."

Soon the network was airing more complex one-hour documentaries on various subjects under such brand names as *MSNBC Investigates.* That approach yielded respectable ratings during slow news periods, but as staffers soon realized, it did nothing to promote MSNBC's identity as a news network. During breaking news, viewers increasingly turned to Fox News or CNN instead of MSNBC.

"The problem, we learned, was that we [were] no longer competing against CNN and Fox in that [breaking news] world," Griffin says. "We were competing with the numerous channels that were putting on documentaries."

By summer 2000, when the political parties staged their national conventions, it was clear that MSNBC was in trouble. Viewers in search of political analysis began gravitating to Fox News, and MSNBC "absolutely tanked" in the ratings, as one former staffer put it. NBC began to treat its cable news channel like a poor relation. "Brian Williams would be kicked off at eight o'clock at night so that Brokaw could come on" for convention coverage, the staffer says. MSNBC was "seen as the puny little cabler that got a .2, which we did." What NBC did not realize at the time was that MSNBC's situation was about to get even worse.

10

The Right Person

"Get out of my studio before I tear you to fucking pieces." —Bill O'Reilly to Jeremy Glick, an antiwar protester whose father died in the September 11 terrorist attacks, in "We Decide, You Shut Up," ***Harper's Magazine,*** May 2003

Barry McCaffrey was angrily shouting in the hallways at Fox News. McCaffrey, the former Gulf War general who served as President Clinton's drug czar, had been invited to discuss America's war on illegal drugs for the premiere of *The O'Reilly Report,* a new Fox talk show hosted by Bill O'Reilly. The general could be forgiven for expecting a softball interview; after all, the network had just launched, and practically no one was watching (the show initially drew no more than thirty thousand viewers, according to one estimate). O'Reilly, best known as the former host of the syndicated tabloid *Inside Edition,* could seemingly ill afford to alienate any big-name guests.

But O'Reilly refused to follow softball rules. He began from the premise that the war on drugs had always been a miserable failure, and it was likely to remain so. "Do you have any plan at all to turn this drug thing around?" he asked.

McCaffrey said the administration had a "national strategy" that emphasized drug prevention and treatment.

"Well, that strategy hasn't worked in the past," O'Reilly retorted, adding that drug use was linked to various social ills including street crime, child abuse, and the spread of AIDS. The general admitted that the government could probably do nothing to stop illegal drugs from entering the country. "You have to treat the root cause," McCaffrey said, sounding more like an idealistic social worker than a battle-hardened military commander.

Off the air minutes later, McCaffrey was livid, ripping into the producer who booked him for the show. "Bill just wasn't taking the standardized answers about the war on drugs," says Fox producer Bill Shine. "I can remember General McCaffrey in the hallway screaming 'cause he can't believe that he got asked those questions and got treated that way. And that was on the first day" of O'Reilly's show. Later, in his best-seller *The No Spin Zone,* O'Reilly rubbed salt in the wound, gleefully writing that the "clueless" general "had walked into an ambush."

McCaffrey was the first of many guests bloodied after a rhetorical encounter with the six-foot-four O'Reilly, a veteran TV reporter variously described by his legion of critics as a bully, a jerk, and a liar. Indeed, topping O'Reilly's lengthy list of grievances were those persons who, for one reason or another, either declined to appear on the show or vowed never to return. The confrontations enhanced the host's self-description as "a journalistic gunslinger"—and eventually propelled *The O'Reilly Factor* to the top of the cable news ratings. After a painfully slow start, O'Reilly gained traction opposite his main rival, CNN's *Larry King Live,* eventually beating that program by a two-to-one margin.

More important, the show became Fox News's signature program and yielded a halo effect for the network's entire prime-time schedule. As O'Reilly is not shy of reminding others, *The Factor* was a key factor in Fox News's overall success. But paving the way for O'Reilly were some critical strategic decisions that ended up recasting viewers' perceptions of TV news.

A large broadcasting company once hired Roger Ailes to evaluate talk-show hosts on its local TV stations. Ailes devised a simple trick to help him decide whether the hosts were any good. He would watch the shows in his hotel room with the sound turned off, closely scrutinizing each host's gestures, facial expressions, and body language with guests. "If there was nothing happening on the screen in the way the host looked or moved that made me interested enough to stand up and turn the sound up, then I knew that the host was not a great television performer," Ailes later wrote.

To Ailes, great television meant great *performances,* whether from a politician, an executive, or a talk-show host. People were the essence of the medium, the reason that viewers watched in the first place. That was Ailes's guiding principle at CNBC, where he signed such idiosyncratic hosts as Chris Matthews, Charles Grodin, and Geraldo Rivera. (It is not coincidental that all three had idiosyncratic styles and were frequent targets of parody on NBC's *Saturday Night Live.*) He expanded on the theme at Fox News, minting two bankable stars in O'Reilly and Sean Hannity, plus a large supporting cast of recognizable anchors and commentators: Alan Colmes, Brit Hume, Shepard Smith, Tony Snow, and so on.

"If I have any ability, it's probably to find talented people and set up a structure that they can work in," Ailes says. "I look for authenticity in people. I don't look for formats to stuff people in. I try to find authenticity and then develop a show from it." Focusing on personalities may sound like a simple insight; after all, commercial TV has depended on stars since the late 1940s. But the Ailes approach would come to revolutionize cable news.

In the early days of CNN, Ted Turner had insisted that "news is the star." While certain newscasters there developed cult followings, such as Headline News's Lynne Russell, it was clear that what distinguished CNN was its roving camera, which seemed to span the entire globe twenty-four hours a day. The anchors were mostly low-profile yeomen—Natalie Allen, Bobbie Battista, Don Farmer, and so on—whose principal role was to provide verbal glue between the video reports. Even when Rick Kaplan was hired in 1997 to refashion CNN's prime-time lineup into "appointment viewing," the emphasis was on dramatic storytelling and improved sets and graphics, not developing star hosts.

Ailes found such an approach misguided, at least for cable TV. "I do think you can create appointment television," Ailes told one reporter, "but it's the people. It may not make a difference whether or not the network looks better. In the end, you may get better ratings if you just have two people sitting in chairs, if you have the right two people."

Prior to the launch of Fox News, Ailes reviewed hundreds of tapes sent by TV journalists from all over the country. Some help in winnowing the pile came from his old boss.

"I think I listened to maybe four hundred or five hundred tapes before we hired the people," says Chet Collier, who had hired Ailes as a production assistant on *The Mike Douglas Show* more than thirty years earlier. "I would listen to the tapes and screen them and bring them to Roger, and the two of us would talk about who we wanted to hire."

A curmudgeonly veteran of TV syndication—a brutally competitive backwater of broadcasting—Collier was probably the person most responsible for Ailes's view of television. He agreed with media philosopher Marshall McLuhan that the relatively small size of the screen necessarily made television a personal and intimate medium. "People tune in to watch somebody, or they tune them out," says Collier.

Despite their ideological differences—Collier is a self-professed liberal who has little use for Ailes's right-wing politics—the pair kept in close touch long after Ailes left *Mike Douglas.* Collier had been in charge of prime-time programming at CNBC under Ailes, and after Fox News was announced, Ailes tapped his old mentor as senior vice president of programming.

To fill the Fox News airwaves, Collier was not necessarily looking for the best journalists. In fact, he spent little time worrying about journalistic quality at all. That was the role carved out for John Moody, the network's vice president for news. Collier tended to view reporters and producers with a mix of amusement and frustration; they were, in his mildly disparaging phrase, "newsies." Like his protégé Ailes, Collier was first and foremost an entertainer. "My job," he says, "was to see that [news] was presented with the most excitement."

Collier believed that "excitement" in news, as in entertainment, depended mainly on writing and casting. "You use the best elements of the entertainment world, and you present news in that package," he says. "That's true of any television show. If you do a documentary, a situation comedy, you take the best material you can get and it damn well better be well written. . . . And you cast it with the best possible people because people watch television because of the individuals that they see on the screen."

That approach made some Fox staffers uncomfortable, but Collier offered no apologies for trying to engage viewers. "It was always a balance between what is the news and what is entertainment—or entertaining," he says. "Of course, the newsies all go crazy when you say that, 'cause essentially you're corrupting a great institution or some bullshit. But you know, you have to get people's attention if you're gonna get any ratings, 'cause you don't want to end up like MSNBC."

The desire to make the news entertaining pushed Fox News toward bright studio lighting, colorful graphics, and attention-grabbing sound effects such as the "swoosh" that accompanied screen wipes. But the emphasis was always on finding stars, and before long the network had found a big one.

A few months after Fox News launched, a frustrated O'Reilly paid a visit to Roger Ailes. *The O'Reilly Report* was airing in the 6 P.M. slot and was having trouble breaking out in the ratings. "It wasn't working very well," Ailes admits.

O'Reilly told Ailes he felt the show should be doing much better.

"Bill, I think I made the mistake," Ailes said. "I think I put you in the wrong time period."

Ailes reasoned that most viewers at 6 P.M. were still learning the day's headlines. They were not ready to hear political opinion, particularly strong opinion like O'Reilly's, which tended toward the stridently populist.

In the early '90s, when he was at *Inside Edition,* O'Reilly was inspired by the success of Rush Limbaugh, who at the time was doing a syndicated TV show (briefly produced by Ailes). "I'm not sure where the business is going," O'Reilly told a friend, "but my gut says it's going in the direction of Rush, and, man, I'm going to be there."

O'Reilly pitched the executives at King World (which distributed *Inside Edition*) a show that resembled an edgy, opinionated version of *Nightline.* After they passed, O'Reilly, who had a long history of tangles with management at ABC News and the numerous stations where he worked earlier in his career, quit the show. He enrolled at the Kennedy School of Government at Harvard, acquiring a master's in public administration in 1996. While in Cambridge he refined his ideas for a new show, eventually pitching it to Ailes, who was just beginning to staff Fox News.

Ailes had already met O'Reilly several times before, once booking him as a guest on his America's Talking show *Straight Forward*. "During that interview I realized, this is a guy with solid journalistic credentials. He's been out on the street for twenty-three years pounding down stories, but he also has strong opinions and is appealing in a kind of likable Irishman way. So that stuck in my mind." When O'Reilly approached Ailes about his show idea, he was invited to Fox News for an interview.

O'Reilly was clear about the type of show he wanted to do. "Every newspaper in the country has an op-ed page and an editorial page, but broadcasters are afraid to do that," O'Reilly says. "I'm not. I think people will be interested to hear opinion, especially after you get the news and you want to know what people think about it. So we took those Sunday morning shows, which do give some opinion—not much, but some—and jazzed it up to the nth degree."

When it became clear that *The O'Reilly Report* was not catching on at 6 P.M., Ailes switched the program to 8 P.M. when the news audience is somewhat younger and more willing to take a chance on a show that goes beyond the headlines. O'Reilly stopped booking authors and entertainers, and focused almost entirely on politics. The result was a unique format in cable news.

"The show was a little softer in the beginning than it is now," O'Reilly says. "We kind of did fifty-fifty hard news and features, because at six o'clock your audience is a little bit older. The demographic that you're going for is more retired people and people who are home early."

The program's name was also changed, to *The O'Reilly Factor.* At the time, nearly all of the Fox shows were called "reports." Ailes and O'Reilly both believed that the 8 P.M. show needed a more distinctive name, though each insists he came up with the *Factor* moniker first. "We fight over that every day," Ailes says.

Whatever the name, O'Reilly had little doubt that the show would work. "I'm not a big kind of doubt guy," he says—an understatement if there ever was one. He writes virtually all the copy ("It's got to have my voice," he says) and structures the show like a magazine, with six segments illuminated by plenty of graphics. *The Factor* kicks off with a Talking Points memo in which the host offers his take on a top news story. The Most Ridiculous Item of the Day is a rant that uses a news tidbit as a launching pad. The program concludes with viewer mail, usually divided more or less evenly between O'Reilly worshippers and haters.

But it was the confrontations that really made *The Factor* take off. O'Reilly does gladiatorial battle every night in his self-proclaimed "No Spin Zone," and viewers turn up to see which miscreant will be tossed to the lions. Actress and liberal activist Susan Sarandon, a frequent O'Reilly punching bag, appeared on *The Factor,* for example, to debate the police shooting of unarmed immigrant Amadou Diallo. O'Reilly argued that aggressive policing in New York, where the shooting occurred, had led to a drop in violent crime. The tension grew as Sarandon insisted that O'Reilly was viewing the problem through the blinkered perspective of a white man.

"I don't see black neighborhoods terrorized," O'Reilly interjected.

"Well, you should go to a black neighborhood," the actress said.

"I have, many, many times," he replied.

After O'Reilly dismissed her, Sarandon ripped the microphone from her blouse and angrily asked the producers, "What's his problem?"

In these battles, the host became a stand-in for the little guy. The Fox News Web site points out that O'Reilly "continues to live on Long Island where his best friends are guys with whom he attended first grade." The implication is that *The Factor* host has not forgotten where he came from—he's still a man of the people. That's a valuable image for a "journalistic gunslinger," even if his former classmates are unlikely to match his $6 million-a-year salary.

In 2000, as the presidential race headed toward a chaotic postelection showdown, O'Reilly published his bestselling *The O'Reilly Factor* and became a cable news phenomenon. Chet Collier had nothing to worry about. Fox News would not end up like MSNBC.

11

Electoral Follies

"In my heart I do believe that democracy was harmed by my network and others on November 7, 2000. I do believe that the great profession of journalism took many steps backward." Roger Ailes, appearing before a 2001 House Committee on the networks' election coverage

Shortly before midnight on November 7, 2000, John Moody sat in the newsroom and stared in disbelief at the latest election returns. "Is this headed the way I think it is?" he asked.

John Ellis, an election consultant hired to help Fox News crunch the numbers, nodded. "It's turning Bush's way," Ellis said.

Pollsters had predicted a close race, although no one foresaw the particular lunacy of this election. Relying on data that appeared to show Vice President Al Gore scoring an upset victory in Florida, many TV networks had confidently projected him as the winner over the Republican contender, George W. Bush. Fox had called Florida for Gore at 7:52 P.M. But now the late returns indicated that the contest was much closer than it had initially seemed. The Fox News team began scrutinizing the Florida numbers. Increasingly it looked as though the presidency would hinge on the outcome in a single state.

Around 2 A.M., Ellis approached Moody and said, "John, based on these numbers, Bush can't lose. He can't lose Florida." No other network had yet called the race. If Fox News did so, it would be the first, and other media would likely follow suit. Moody told Ellis and the other three members of the election team to sit down and go over the numbers one more time. After a few minutes, the other team members agreed that Gore did not have a chance of carrying the state.

Fox called the election for Bush at 2:16 A.M. Within two minutes, NBC, CBS, and CNN had done the same. Word came that Gore had conceded the race in a personal phone call to Bush. The media awaited a formal concession speech at the Gore headquarters in Nashville so that Bush could then appear before supporters to claim victory.

But the minutes passed, and Gore never showed up. Moody later recalled feeling queasy when it was revealed that Gore had phoned Bush again to retract his concession. Just then, around 3 A.M., Ellis called Moody over and said the Florida numbers were changing again.

"You said they couldn't," Moody said.

Ellis replied, "I was wrong."

What followed was a bitter six-week electoral wrangle that divided the country and deepened partisan debate. Fox News played a high-profile role in the election battle, especially over Ellis and his controversial call. But there was little disputing that beginning with President Clinton's impeachment and culminating in the chaotic 2000 election that followed, the network found its voice and began rising to the top of the ratings. Domestic politics, which had suffered from a lack of epic stories since Clarence Thomas's contentious Supreme Court confirmation hearings in the early 1990s, began stirring the interest of viewers again, and Fox was uniquely positioned to tap into their frustrations with the mainstream media while maintaining its often irreverent and personality-driven style.

In retrospect, what Gulf War I was to CNN, the impeachment and 2000 election were to Fox News.

"This is about alleged criminal activity of the most serious kind," Bill O'Reilly intoned, wagging his omnipresent pen at the camera, "and President and Mrs. Clinton are the focus."

In his "Talking Points" segment for January 27, 1999, *The Factor* host was blasting the Clintons not over the president's affair with White House intern Monica Lewinsky, but for their ties to indicted former Justice Department official Webster Hubbell, who had received hundreds of thousands of dollars in questionable gifts and fees from sources sympathetic to the White House. "All Americans should demand to know why Webb Hubbell was paid nearly $1 million for little or no work and why [Clinton friend] Vernon Jordan was involved," O'Reilly told viewers.

O'Reilly, Fox News's biggest star, had turned into a reliable voice for the sizable minority that had grown to loathe the forty-second president of the United States. As the host wrote in his best-seller, *The O'Reilly Factor,* "The much-publicized affair with Monica Lewinsky was trivial (except to Hillary and Chelsea). What was *not* trivial was [Clinton's] lying about the whole thing, which paralyzed the nation's executive and legislative branches for more than a year."

Critics could not accuse Fox News of leading the way in reporting on the Lewinsky scandal or the impeachment drama that followed. Other media played that role, including Internet scribe Matt Drudge (who was later briefly hired by Fox News as an on-air host) and *Newsweek,* whose investigative reporter Michael Isikoff scored a number of attention-grabbing scoops. Many of the pundits who sharply criticized or denounced President Clinton from the outset, in fact, worked for mainstream, supposedly left-leaning media organizations, such as ABC's Sam Donaldson and Cokie Roberts and *The Washington Post*'s David Broder and Sally Quinn.

What Fox News did provide was a steady drumbeat of analysis and opinion, much of it broadly directed against the Clintons. After luring Brit Hume away from ABC News the previous year, Fox News seemed somewhat at a loss how to use him until the Lewinsky scandal came along; the need to give viewers regular updates on the Oval Office fiasco resulted in *Special Report with Brit Hume.*

On September 11, 1998—the day that special prosecutor Kenneth Starr issued his report followed by a public apology from President Clinton—conservative commentator Mort Kondracke launched a blistering attack during a Fox News roundtable with Hume. "What strikes me at the end of the day is that the president starts out by saying, 'I have sinned and I repent.' Then comes the defense. And what is the defense? The defense is a lie. . . . The one person [Clinton] hasn't apologized to is Ken Starr. . . . Clearly, Ken Starr had a job to do, and he did it, and Bill Clinton tried to thwart him at every turn."

Some Fox staffers complained that even in its news coverage the network was anything but "fair and balanced." Jed Duvall, an ex-ABC News reporter, said, "I'll never forget the morning that one producer came up to me and, rubbing her hands like Uriah Heep, said, 'Let's have something on Whitewater today.' That sort of thing doesn't happen at a professional news organization." Duvall ended up quitting the network after a year.

Another broadcast veteran, former CBS producer Don Dahler, quit the network after claiming he was ordered to soften a report which showed that, despite the economic boom, black Americans still lagged in social gains. *Columbia Journalism Review,* a frequent Fox News critic, wrote of several former Fox staffers who "complained of 'management sticking their fingers' in the writing and editing of stories to cook the facts to make a story more palatable to right-of-center tastes."

Ailes and other Fox News officials pointed to the fact that the roundtables and opinion shows were regularly balanced with liberal commentators, such as Hannity sidekick Alan Colmes and National Public Radio's Mara Liasson. Yet as journalist Marshall Sella wrote, "On an average news day, Fox News leans to the right just as CNN leans to the left. Besides the conservative lilt of the evening talk shows—which, granted, are opinion shows—it doesn't take an electron microscope to see that FNC is a haven if not for conservatism then at least for conservatives."

Competitors noticed that, with the impeachment, Ailes and company were beginning to connect with viewers. By the time Clinton was acquitted in February 1999, Fox News had narrowed a once formidable gap with number two MSNBC. Fox News "got an enormous lift . . . beginning probably with the Clinton hearings in Congress, with Monica Lewinsky," says NBC chief Bob Wright. "They struck a chord with O'Reilly in particular, and Hannity and Colmes next—they struck a chord with the public who was anxious to strike out at what the public felt was an atrocity happening in the White House. There was a great release of energy, and Fox found that handle."

While Fox surfed on the wave of anger directed at the Clintons, the network also undoubtedly benefited from the troubles that continued to torment its competitors. As the Clinton scandal and impeachment began dominating the news, Ted Turner's news network was still trying to recover its footing from the Tailwind debacle.

At the heart of the struggle was *NewsStand,* the ballyhooed magazine show that had launched with the ill-fated Tailwind story. CNN/US chief Rick Kaplan remained a big believer in the series, despite the fact that it did little to boost ratings. In fact, Kaplan expanded *NewsStand,* which was conceived as a weekly series, to five nights a week at 10 P.M. starting in mid-1999. Big stories such as the war in Yugoslavia and the death of John F. Kennedy Jr. forced the program to accommodate breaking news at the top of the broadcast, but *NewsStand*'s focus remained the sort of taped magazine pieces that were Kaplan's specialty.

Network insiders griped that *NewsStand* had turned into an expensive flop. The series plowed through an estimated $40 million during its first year with hardly any ratings benefit. Many staffers agreed with CNN chairman Tom Johnson that, Tailwind aside, *NewsStand* was generally well produced, but a consensus developed that Kaplan was following a doomed plan. He saw his real competition as ABC, CBS, and NBC, not Fox News and MSNBC. Kaplan grew to loathe the graphs on display at CNN Center that showed the network's ratings spiking during big news events and then dropping precipitously during periods of calm. The charts were a reminder that CNN was less like a network than a utility whose usage soared only during crises. The main thrust of Kaplan's job was to give CNN better ratings even when there were no major breaking stories. But critics argued that his broadcast mentality did nothing to address the growing ratings threat posed by cable competitors. Fox News and MSNBC were, after all, jockeying for the same ad dollars as CNN. Kaplan was learning, just as his counterparts at MSNBC were, that cable news is a very different beast than broadcast.

"I think Rick was [of the] *World News Tonight* school of news: If you spend enough money on the product, you can bring 16 million people to watch it," says former CNN executive Steve Haworth. "But I don't think CNN will ever have 16 million people [watching] unless the world is ending."

Kaplan admitted that some of the more feature-oriented *NewsStand* collaborations with Time Warner magazines may have turned off CNN's core audience of news junkies. "With *Entertainment Weekly* and *Fortune,* for example, those would have done amazingly well on a broadcast network, but they didn't work with the CNN viewer tuning in for breaking news," he told a reporter. "I thought I could do a monolithic hour [of magazine pieces]. . . . This is my error."

Even on breaking stories, Kaplan's news judgment was sometimes faulted. Technology stocks at the time were enjoying a huge run-up, and

Kaplan believed that viewers were devouring breaking business news the same way they once followed Cold War–related political and foreign stories. But when he tried to inject more financial news into CNN's coverage, some staffers complained that the network was straying from its mandate and cannibalizing CNNfn, Turner's rival to CNBC.

Despite the criticisms, Time Warner kept showering money on the network, which was still a reliable profit center. Kaplan oversaw a $7.5 million remodeling of the newsroom and anchor desk, yielding a sleek and colorful on-air backdrop. Kaplan and Johnson agreed that many of CNN's ratings woes were due to a lack of promotion, so the company spent $20 million for a major advertising push—astonishingly the first such campaign in the network's history.

Alas, promotion was one of the few topics on which Kaplan and his boss found common ground. While the relationship between the two men had never been warm, in the aftermath of the Tailwind scandal it grew positively poisonous. Johnson, who tried at all times to maintain the decorum of a southern gentleman, was publicly supportive of his lieutenant, although sometimes that support was expressed through gritted teeth. He concedes that Kaplan was, after Lou Dobbs, the most difficult executive he ever attempted to manage. CNN staffers were baffled that the chairman remained in Kaplan's corner even after the Tailwind disaster. "Many criticized me for sticking with Rick Kaplan," Johnson says. "I felt then and continue to believe he is a brilliant producer." Even so, he adds, "Many of the CNN veterans turned on Rick. The Tailwind fiasco had weakened him."

Johnson had stood by besieged executives before—for instance, saving Lou Dobbs from Ted Turner's ax after it was revealed that the *Moneyline* anchor had done promotional videos for companies he reported on. Yet Kaplan was no more grateful to Johnson than Dobbs had been. Kaplan grew contemptuous of Johnson's management style, which he found plodding and timid. That was especially true in the months following Tailwind, when even some Johnson backers noticed that the CNN chairman had become gun-shy about any story that smacked of controversy. Kaplan concluded to associates that Johnson "wanted to be loved; he didn't want to lead."

In mid-August 2000, the parking lot outside Staples Center in downtown Los Angeles was a crowded harbor of trailers, satellite trucks, and antennae. The media had descended on the city to cover the Democratic National Convention, but the broadcast networks—which had been steadily paring back their political coverage for years—were almost an afterthought. The real TV news rivalry was between CNN and the surging Fox News, which had not even been on the air during the previous presidential election.

CNN spared little for its gavel-to-gavel coverage; Larry King broadcast live from a booth overlooking the convention floor, as did anchor Judy Woodruff and analyst Jeff Greenfield. Tom Johnson and his favorite lieutenant, Eason Jordan, personally oversaw much of the coverage, pecking away at laptops in a cramped makeshift news bureau inside Staples Center. Political notables such as Senate Democratic leader Tom Daschle dropped by for hosted chats on CNN.com.

Amid all the hoopla, though, Fox kept nipping at its rival's heels. The network's PR department reminded reporters of CNN's close ties to the Democratic Party: Johnson had worked for President Johnson, while Clinton pal Rick Kaplan had slept in the Lincoln Bedroom. A sweaty and rumpled Bill O'Reilly hunched his towering frame over a computer in the Fox trailer, writing copy for each night's *Factor,* at the same time complaining to anyone who would listen that Gore and other notable Democrats were too afraid to appear on his show.

CNN executives publicly shrugged off Fox, but behind the scenes they were put on the defensive by their competitor's broadsides. Fox News had turned in an astonishingly strong performance two weeks earlier during the Republican National Convention in Philadelphia. During May 2000, Fox News still trailed MSNBC in average viewers over a twenty-four-hour period, 135,000 versus 155,000; CNN averaged 249,000 viewers. But during the GOP convention, Fox's ratings soared and at key times even surpassed CNN's. The numbers for Fox wilted during the Democrats' confab—which many pundits took as evidence of FNC's rightward tilt—but the convention numbers still amounted to a shot across CNN's bow.

Fox officials viewed the conventions— accurately, as it turned out—as a chance to demonstrate to viewers that their coverage was indeed different from what turned up on other networks. "When your motto and creed and pledge to viewers is fair and balanced news, it's not easy to show when you're covering fires and floods and train wrecks," Hume told a reporter just before the Democratic convention. "By and large, when you show fairness and balance is when [you're] covering political stories."

Earlier that summer, with Fox News and CNN heading for a showdown, Rick Kaplan boldly predicted that CNN would be the "network of record" for the election. Long before that forecast could be realized, however, Kaplan was out. Just days after the Democratic convention wrapped in Los Angeles, Kaplan sat looking at a revised management chart for the network and realized that his name was nowhere to be found. Kaplan's three-year experiment to help CNN compete against its new cable rivals was officially over.

Earlier that year, at the height of the Internet frenzy, Time Warner chief Jerry Levin had unveiled a $160 billion merger with online services giant AOL, in a combination billed as the ultimate junction of old and new media. New management at Turner Broadcasting, hoping to get CNN's house in order prior to the official close of the deal, ordered a sweeping review of the network, which incidentally was celebrating its twentieth anniversary. Tom Johnson called the review process "very painful and very exhaustive." The evaluation was led personally by Terry McGuirk, a longtime Turner insider tapped as the new chairman of Turner Broadcasting, as well as new TBS president Steve Heyer, a former management consultant. But the driving force behind the review appeared to be AOL executive Bob Pittman, who would assume ultimate authority over CNN once the merger was completed.

McGuirk and Heyer concluded that CNN needed fresh leadership, the sooner the better. In addition to jettisoning Kaplan, they stripped Johnson of his business and operational roles. Those duties were assigned to Phil Kent, a former agent at Hollywood powerhouse CAA (Creative Artists Agency), who would report directly to Heyer. "I was left primarily with news gathering only," Johnson says.

The network struggled to put the best face on the moves. "This change [with] Rick was not about ratings," Johnson told a reporter. Yet it was obvious that executives at Time Warner were growing increasingly concerned about the growing threat from Fox, particularly its outstanding performance during the Republican convention that summer. Joining Kaplan on the casualty list was his prime-time magazine *NewsStand,* which had never broken out in the ratings.

Kaplan went on to teach at Harvard before finally rejoining ABC News to help lead the network's coverage of Gulf War II. Johnson was not so lucky. He was ousted completely from CNN in 2001 when the network underwent yet another wrenching management overhaul.

Less than three weeks after the 2000 election, Florida's Secretary of State Katherine Harris certified results showing that Bush had carried the state. Fox News was the only network that accepted the certification as determining the presidency, with a graphic announcing FLORIDA DECISION. The other networks continued to hedge the outcome until at least December 12, when the U.S. Supreme Court reversed a Florida court order mandating manual recounts in certain counties. The following day Gore conceded.

Brit Hume believed that other networks' down-the-middle coverage gave Fox News a chance to connect with alienated Republicans. "My thought about [the Gore camp's challenge of the results] was that Republicans in particular were going to be incredibly outraged by this, that they were going to see this as the refusal of the Democrats to accept the rules of the election as they were and [that Democrats] were going to try to get them changed," Hume says. "The media, by and large, did not cover it that way; it simply treated it as an open-ended, fifty-fifty dispute."

Fox News took its two top political reporters, Jim Angle and Carl Cameron, off the Bush and Gore campaigns and dispatched them to Florida to interpret court decisions and recount results. As the battle raged, Fox News anchor John Gibson commented on the air, "I think what's going on is the Democratic lawyers have flooded Florida. They are afraid of George W. Bush becoming president and instituting tort reform and their gravy train will be over. This is the trial association's full court press to make sure Bush does not win."

This type of coverage was music to the ears of conservatives who believed that the rest of the media were Democratic-controlled and strongly tipped toward Gore's recount quest. "There was a very large audience that had given up on network news, CNN and the [broadcast] networks included, and hadn't watched for years," Hume says. "But this story to them was so compelling and so suspenseful that they were tuning in and looking for something to watch and they found us. We picked up tremendously [in the ratings] during that Florida recount." It was during the recount battle, in fact, when Fox News began regularly defeating MSNBC in total viewership. For the month of November 2000, Fox News averaged just over 1 million viewers in prime time, compared to 1.6 million for CNN and 756,000 for MSNBC. From that point forward, Fox News began redirecting its energies away from battling MSNBC and toward toppling CNN.

The electoral map had been divided into pro-Bush "red states," largely in the center of the country, and "blue states," mostly on the coasts, that went for Gore. Fox News left little doubt at which states its coverage was aimed. "There's a whole country that elitists will never acknowledge," Ailes later told *The New York Times.* "What people deeply resent out there are those in the 'blue' states thinking they're smarter. There's a touch of that [resentment] in our news."

Even when Fox News was besieged by complaints of bias in its coverage of the election, it shrewdly redirected the attacks to point an accusing finger at its rivals. A few days after the election, with a recount battle shaping up, it was reported that Fox consultant John Ellis had relayed early vote totals on election night to both George W. Bush and his brother, Florida governor Jeb Bush. What particularly complicated Ellis's role is that he is a first cousin to the Bush brothers.

Gore supporters argued, credibly enough, that Ellis's premature decision to call the race for Bush had spurred competitors to do the same and, despite later retractions, fostered perceptions that the Republicans had won long before officials could sort out the mess. A Gore spokesman said there were "serious questions" about Ellis's role in the election.

Ellis denied that he had improperly shared confidential information with the Bushes, but Fox News still appeared to be facing the sort of conflict-of-interest problem that could erupt into a journalistic scandal. The fact that a few days before the election Fox News had broken the story of Bush's once being arrested for drunken driving did little to dispel the controversy. Moody and other Fox News executives were well aware of Ellis's connections but never believed the election would be so close as to make his family tree relevant. "I will bet that any of the network polling analysts will tell you that a perfect storm like 2000 only comes up once in a while," Moody says. "We were screwed before this [Ellis controversy] ever got started."

But support soon came from a high place. Speaking to reporters after a shareholders' meeting, Rupert Murdoch defended Ellis, pointing out that he had worked as a consultant to NBC in three prior presidential elections without any complaints. The remarks took the focus off Ellis's family ties and implied that what really upset critics was not the consultant's alleged conflict of interest but, rather, Fox's early call for Bush.

Ari Fleischer, the Bush campaign spokesman, sounded that theme as well, echoing Fox News's reminders that CNN was led by executives with close ties to Democrats. "The media is full of people who are very close to candidates," Fleischer said. "The exception is to be close to a Republican. The norm is to be close to a Democrat."

Much of the controversy over the networks' chaotic election coverage was centered on Voter News Service, a consortium that provided poll data to the media (VNS was later disbanded). Appearing at a February 2001 House committee hearing on election night coverage, Roger Ailes admitted that "Fox News, along with all the other television networks, made errors . . . which cannot be repeated." Ailes noted that following the election debacle, Fox News had promised not to call future races in a state until all the polls had closed. But he also vigorously defended his longtime friend Ellis, whom he called a "consummate professional." "Obviously, through his family connections, Mr. Ellis has very good sources," Ailes told the committee. "I do not see this as a fault or shortcoming of Mr. Ellis. Quite the contrary, I see this as a good journalist talking to his very high level sources on election night." Ailes added that two other members of the election team, John Gorman and Arnon Mishkin, had been on the phone with Democratic sources the entire evening.

With the end of the Clinton era and the ascendancy of another Bush to the Oval Office, Fox News's success was beginning to put liberals in a despairing frame of mind. Susan Estrich—a Fox News contributor and former adviser to Democrat Michael Dukakis's failed 1988 presidential campaign—lamented to *The Nation* in early 2001: "Where are these guys on the left who can do a news channel that covers the news well and also provides an opportunity to get their views across?"

12

Waving the Flag

"Look, we understand the enemy—they've made themselves clear: they want to murder us. We don't sit around and get all gooey and wonder if these people have been misunderstood in their childhood. If they're going to try to kill us, that's bad." —Roger Ailes on the September 11 terrorists, ***The New York Times,*** December 3, 2001

At Fox News headquarters in midtown Manhattan, news chief John Moody conducts meetings with his senior producers every morning and afternoon. He was in the middle of the 8:30 meeting on September 11, 2001, when an image of smoke billowing from the World Trade Center popped up on the monitor in the conference room.

"Oh my God, look at that," someone said.

A producer in the Washington bureau, who had been pitching a story via speakerphone about scandal-plagued Congressman Gary Condit, muttered, "Well, nothing else matters now."

Staffers cleared out to cover the story, although at that moment no one had any idea how big the story was. Minutes later, Moody was standing in the newsroom when live cameras caught a second plane, a United Airlines jet, plowing into the South Tower.

In the Fox News studio, anchor Jon Scott had taken over from the morning program *Fox & Friends.* A few minutes after the second tower was hit, Scott speculated to viewers about who might be responsible for the attacks, adding, "The name that has to come to mind is Osama Bin Laden"—perhaps the first time a national news anchor openly linked the attacks to Al Qaeda.

Like staffers at all of the networks, Moody and his crew were just gearing up for what would become a bleary-eyed, sixty-hour marathon of news coverage. "I don't think I came up to my office all day that day," Moody says. Rupert Murdoch, who was headed back to New York after a trip to Washington, could not get back into the city due to bridge and tunnel closures, and ended up spending the night at Roger Ailes's house in New Jersey. Ailes, meanwhile, was stuck in his office, where he took catnaps on a sofa.

The day was filled with so much news—virtually all of it shocking and immensely sad—that Fox News was forced to introduce an innovation that soon became standard on cable. A "crawl"—a line of text scrolling across the bottom of the screen—began carrying continuous updates, much like the stock ticker on CNBC. "By the end of the day," Moody says, "we realized that there was just too much information to keep repeating the top of the story over and over." Soon the crawl appeared on CNN and MSNBC as well.

Everyone quickly realized that the attacks would entail some life-altering changes. What no one knew in the rush to make sense of that chaotic day was that the attacks would mark a turning point in the cable news race. That was in no small part because of some on-air decisions made by Fox News. In the aftermath of September 11, many viewers seemed to perceive Fox News differently, and many discovered the network for the first time. But that was not the only change. CNN was once again struggling with behind-the-scenes turmoil.

Paula Zahn, who had undergone an ugly split from Fox News just the week before, found her way that morning to CNN's New York bureau at 5 Penn Plaza. An experienced anchor, Zahn was not even scheduled to start working for her new employer for six months. In the interim she was planning a lengthy vacation interspersed with visits to the network's far-flung bureaus. She was spending the morning at home when she learned of the attacks, whereupon she tried frantically to reach her husband, real estate executive Richard Cohen, who was in a meeting across the street at 110 Liberty when the first plane hit.

After being reassured by Cohen's office that he was safe and would pick up their children from school, she next rang Walter Isaacson, also a newcomer to CNN. A highly esteemed magazine editor and author, he had been hired over the summer as the network's new president, and hopes were high that he would manage to turn around the channel's sagging fortunes.

Zahn told Isaacson that she wanted to do something to help cover the story. Isaacson thought for a moment and told her to head over to the bureau. Zahn had almost hung up the phone before she realized that she didn't even know where the CNN bureau was. About an hour later, Zahn walked into the Penn Plaza office and was hurled into a maelstrom. "From the time I walked in the bureau to the time I went on the air was maybe fifteen minutes, interfacing with hundreds of people I'd never met before," she says.

For the rest of the day, Zahn anchored CNN's coverage of the disaster with another new face, Aaron Brown, formerly of ABC News. The pair stood on the bureau's rooftop, updating viewers on the disaster as the wreck of the Twin Towers sent plumes of black smoke across the skyline to the south. CNN would end up averaging nearly 8 million viewers for the day, or more than ten times the usual number.

The attacks came at a perilous time for CNN. With the competitive threat growing daily, Ted Turner's news network was once again grappling with its chronic identity crisis.

In January, following regulatory approval, online services giant AOL had completed its $106 billion merger with Time Warner, creating the world's largest media company. At the time, the deal was pitched as the ultimate junction of old and new media. Time Warner's powerful content—magazines, movies, and TV shows—would be unleashed on AOL's 26 million paid subscribers. And networks like CNN could help promote Internet services in much the same way that Bill Gates and Jack Welch promised MSNBC would do five years earlier. "We think it's a world of convergence," AOL chief Steve Case told reporters.

Unfortunately, the new merger meant a painful round of companywide layoffs, and CNN was not spared. In late January the network shed four hundred jobs, or nearly 10 percent of its staff. Among those shown the door were correspondent Jim Moret, who led the coverage of the O. J. Simpson trial in 1995, and Washington-based anchor Gene Randall, a seventeen-year CNN veteran. One employee described the mood at CNN Center as like a funeral home. Fired staffers were led to a room on the eleventh floor, where they were told to hand in their company badges and given a folder outlining their severance benefits. "You're picking your jaw off the floor," said laid-off videotape editor Christie Reff, a sixteen-year network veteran.

Demoralizing as the layoffs were, survivors may have faced an even more difficult challenge in the following months. In March, Jamie Kellner, a seasoned television executive who founded the WB Network and helped start the Fox Broadcasting Company, became the new chief of Turner Broadcasting. Kellner's empire would include not only the Turner entertainment networks, such as TNT and Cartoon Network, but also CNN, Headline News, and other all-news operations. To many CNN veterans, this was an ominous development. As they never tired of pointing out, Kellner was worse than just a nonjournalist; he was a slick Hollywood salesman with a broadcast (read: lowest common denominator) mentality. Kellner arrived with a mandate to shake up CNN and the other Turner networks, which AOL's senior management believed had grown somewhat stale. Around the time the merger cleared, AOL's Bob Pittman set up a lunch date with Kellner, who at that time was still running the WB.

"Pittman . . . said he felt that they needed some new creative thinking about the networks, especially CNN," Kellner says. "I said I would look at the channels and give him my thoughts about it." After carefully watching the networks, Kellner agreed there was plenty of room for improvement. "CNN, I thought, had a lot of work that needed to be done in terms of presentation and in terms of the journalists who were appearing on air, the anchors," he says. "The promotion was almost nonexistent, and the on-air look was very dated." His complaints, in fact, sounded very similar to those of Rick Kaplan, who had been pushed out as the president of CNN's domestic network the previous summer.

When TBS chief Terry McGuirk resigned weeks later, Pittman again approached Kellner, who said he would relocate to Atlanta and take the job for two years, "and if I liked it, I would stay longer," Kellner says.

Kellner moved quickly with a plan to rejuvenate CNN. To assist in the effort he brought along Garth Ancier, a longtime lieutenant who had just been ousted as the entertainment president at NBC. The pair began focusing intently on the on-air look of CNN, especially the anchors and correspondents.

"We started doing talent meetings where we'd go through [the correspondents' roster] and say, 'Who's good journalistically and who's good television?'" Ancier says. "'If [they] don't have both these skills, why are they here?'"

Kellner decided to rehire Lou Dobbs, who had left two years earlier after the nasty on-air spat with Kaplan. But the new management agreed that it was critical to find new stars. Many of CNN's most familiar faces, such as Wolf Blitzer and Judy Woodruff, were middle-aged; Larry King was in his late sixties. Bernard Shaw, who became CNN's star anchor thanks to his reporting during the Persian Gulf War, announced his retirement shortly after the AOL Time Warner merger, leaving CNN without a single marquee anchor in prime time. "When we got [to CNN], the operative question was 'Who's going to host this thing in the event of a war?'" Ancier says. "Bernie Shaw was retired, and there was no one else with that kind of gravitas on the network."

Kellner adds, "What you've got to do is build the next generation of stars who are going to eventually grow into these positions."

So in addition to Zahn, Kellner hired the fifty-two-year-old Aaron Brown, who had served as a substitute for Peter Jennings and Ted Koppel at ABC News. In the studio, Kellner and Ancier borrowed a page from Fox News, ordering brighter lighting and more flattering makeup and hairstyling. They mandated quick news updates sprinkled throughout the lineup and ordered sixty-minute programs to start at the top of the hour, rather than sometimes at the half hour as in the past. They turned Headline News, CNN's low-rated sister channel, into a sort of incubator. Headline News was reintroduced in August 2001 with a new on-air look. The screen was filled with bright graphics that at times threatened to blot out the anchor. One critic, echoing many complaints, found Headline News's new look "impossibly cluttered with a dozen or so items."

Kellner insisted the makeover was a step in the right direction. "CNN was run by journalists. Tom Johnson was a print journalist," Kellner says. "Print journalists don't worry about hair and makeup, you know." The irony is that the person picked to be Johnson's replacement under the new Kellner regime—the person tapped to oversee directly

CNN's rejuvenation in the face of the Fox onslaught—was, of all things, a print journalist.

On paper, Walter Isaacson possessed finer news credentials than any other CNN president. Even Kaplan, who had been a star producer at ABC News, had not enjoyed a journalism career as varied and distinguished as Isaacson's. Except for his obvious lack of television experience, the new CNN chief had only one drawback: He did not really want the job.

A New Orleans native, Isaacson was a Harvard grad and Rhodes Scholar. He covered Louisiana politics for the *New Orleans Times-Picayune* and in 1979 joined *Time*, where his sophisticated coverage of Ronald Reagan's White House bid won him favorable attention. During the mid-1990s, Isaacson served as editor of Time Inc.'s new media division and was instrumental in setting up the company's Pathfinder Web service and Roadrunner high-speed data service. He was tapped as managing editor of *Time* in 1996 and quickly became known as an adept "packager" of cover features. At a time when the Internet and twenty-four-hour cable news threatened to make news weeklies obsolete, Isaacson's prized skill was in pulling together elegant and upbeat packages on pop culture, literature, and science.

Staffers stood in awe of Isaacson's line editing skills. "You look at stuff that's gone through his word processor and you say, 'Thank God he looked at it,'" says Fox News's John Moody, who worked at *Time* with Isaacson. "He made my prose sing."

Outside the Time-Life Building, Isaacson was perhaps best known as the author of *Kissinger,* a scrupulously researched biography praised by critics for its evenhanded take on the controversial diplomat. The book attempted to get critical distance on a statesman whose legacy was somewhat obscured by celebrity, although Isaacson did not skimp on gossip. The volume even offered the straight dope on Kissinger's famed romps with actress Jill St. John. Kissinger cut off all communication with his biographer for years, finally burying the hatchet when Isaacson invited the former Secretary of State to a star-studded party celebrating *Times*'s seventy-fifth anniversary. "Well, Walter, even the Seven Years' War had to end at some point," Kissinger told his biographer. "I have forgiven you."

That a newsman with Isaacson's background should be chosen president of CNN was striking. Unlike Burt Reinhardt, Isaacson had a true journalist's temperament. Unlike Tom Johnson, Isaacson was not the sort of person who would wring his hands over a story because it provoked Henry Kissinger's wrath.

Johnson, who had been demoted in 2000, was finally ousted following the AOL merger, and Jerry Levin, CEO of the newly merged AOL Time Warner, was looking for a new CNN chief. Isaacson, as it happened, was looking for a change as well. He had been shifted from managing editor of *Time* to editorial director of the Time Inc. magazines, a largely administrative job that to his mind offered little room for journalistic creativity. "It was not a great job, frankly," he says. "I kind of liked running my own product much more than worrying about whether Carol Wallace was running *People* magazine well."

Levin, along with Kellner and AOL's Bob Pittman, began lobbying Isaacson to take the network job. "It wasn't something I really wanted to do," Isaacson says. "I'm not somebody who had all my life studied and loved television." But Levin and the others would not take no for an answer. Isaacson's sterling credentials and packaging skills, they believed, were just what CNN needed to break out of its rut. "I did it 'cause they were pretty insistent," Isaacson says.

Isaacson was greeted with controversy almost as soon as he took the job. Conservatives had long complained that CNN ignored or even belittled their views, and these critics nurtured a long list of grievances—from the Tailwind saga to alleged editorial neglect of right-wing causes—to bolster their point. The "Clinton News Network" or "Communist News Network" could not be trusted to report fairly, conservatives argued. ("That was before it became the 'Chandra News Network,'" joked columnist Maureen Dowd, referring to relentless cable coverage of the disappearance of an attractive young Washington intern.) House Majority Leader Tom DeLay announced that he was boycotting CNN. Now, with Fox News's ratings growing, CNN appeared to be pursuing a make-nice campaign. *USA Today* reported that CNN was considering a weekend show with right-wing radio host Rush Limbaugh, a story that network insiders charge was planted by Limbaugh himself.

In early August, *Roll Call,* the congressional newspaper, revealed that Isaacson had paid a visit to Capitol Hill for a series of meetings with such Republican leaders as Senator Trent Lott, Speaker of the House Dennis Hastert, and Representative J. C. Watts. The meetings were widely interpreted as a rightward shift for the besieged network. The new CNN chief was "giving the impression that he will sacrifice objectivity to improve ratings," Dowd wrote in *The New York Times.* Democrats dryly noted that Isaacson had not bothered to darken their doorsteps.

Isaacson, perhaps naively, was surprised by the reaction. Framing the talks as mere courtesy visits from "the new kid in town," he says that the media overreacted. Lott complained to Isaacson that anchor Judy Woodruff had misstated some relatively minor facts during an interview, but the Mississippi Republican seemed perturbed mainly that he was not getting enough airtime on CNN.

"If I was worried about getting Trent Lott or others on TV, I realized that I didn't have that trouble," Isaacson says. "The only complaint we may have had was that we weren't putting them on enough."

The upshot of the incident, though, was clear. Its objectivity under attack, now from both the right *and* the left, CNN was once again put on the defensive. "It must have shocked the liberals at CNN when the first two moves Walter made were to visit Trent Lott and call Rush Limbaugh," Roger Ailes cracked to a reporter. "This will be the first time in history a network news president will have to travel with a security detail inside the building."

Within days of the terrorist attacks, viewers who gave Fox News a more than casual glance noticed something unusual in the upper left-hand corner of the frame: an American flag.

With a wave of post-attack patriotism seizing the nation, Rich O'Brien, the network's celebrated graphics chief, toyed around on his computer and came up with an image of a waving Stars and Stripes alternating with the Fox logo. O'Brien showed the graphic to Moody and asked if some viewers might find the image offensive.

"Is it offensive?" Moody repeated. "Rich, I think it's one of the most beautiful things I've ever seen."

"From there on," Moody says, the flag "became our trademark."

Critics could rightly wonder whether, in matching its logo with Old Glory, Fox was equating itself with all things American. And wonder the critics did, but the network made no apologies for wrapping itself in the flag. In the wake of September 11, Fox decided that it was going to take sides, giving "fair and balanced" an elastic meaning. This was not *a* war but *our* war.

When rumors surfaced that CNN had banned the use of the word *terrorist* to describe the hijackers (critics may have confused the network with the wire service Reuters, which did issue such a ban), CNN felt compelled to issue a statement saying that it "has consistently and repeatedly referred to the attackers and hijackers as terrorists, and it will continue to do so."

Fox News had no need of issuing such a statement; *terrorist* was one of the gentler appellations it used for the hijackers. *The New York Times* noted that Fox anchors and commentators had referred to Osama Bin Laden as "a dirtbag" and "a monster" and to Al Qaeda as being comprised of "terror goons." Fox correspondent Geraldo Rivera promised that if he ran across Bin Laden in his Mideast travels, he would kill the terror leader himself. The *Times* observed, "Ever since the terrorist attacks on Sept. 11, the network has become a sort of headquarters for viewers who want their news served up with extra patriotic fervor. In the process, Fox has pushed television news where it has never gone before: to unabashed and vehement support of a war effort, carried in tough-guy declarations often expressing thirst for revenge."

There was little doubt that Fox articulated the anger many Americans felt in the days following the attacks. On September 13, Bill O'Reilly vowed on the air that if the Taliban refused to cooperate with the search for Osama Bin Laden, the Afghan rulers would be "blasted" by U.S. military might. When a guest asked, "Who will you kill in the process?" O'Reilly replied, "Doesn't make any difference."

The network's sense of moral clarity came from the top. On September 14, during a memorial service for terrorist victims at the National Cathedral in Washington, President Bush spoke along with leaders from several religious faiths. John Moody listened with great interest as a Protestant minister said that what had been done to the United States was simply evil. "It did something for me," Moody says of the sermon. "To hear that from a clergyman, that this is evil, this is not just conditional, this is not somebody who's misunderstood, it's not somebody that didn't get Oreos when he was a kid. This is evil. And that helped me make some of the editorial choices that we had to make. People always ask, 'How could you ever say, you know, "us and them" and "our troops" and whatnot?' That [sermon] was part of the decision-making process."

Many viewers clearly approved. Fox's daily ratings surged 43 percent in the wake of the attacks, to nearly 750,000 viewers.

Fox turned aside critics' complaints that the network was trampling on long-sacred traditions of journalistic objectivity. "Suddenly, our competition has discovered 'fair and balanced,'" Ailes told the *Times,* "but only when it's [concerning] radical terrorism versus the United States. I don't believe that democracy and terrorism are relative things you can talk about, and I don't think there's any moral equivalence in those two positions. . . . If that makes me a bad guy, tough luck. I'm still getting the ratings."

13

A Dead Raccoon

"Make her a star . . . then I can get rid of her." —Ted Turner on his mistress Liz Wickersham, a former ***Playboy*** model who served as a CNN host during the early 1980s, in Robert Goldberg and Gerald Jay Goldberg, ***Citizen Turner***

All Greta Van Susteren wanted was a chair. One evening, a month or so after the terrorist attacks of September 11, the talk host arrived at the CNN studio in Washington to do her prime-time show, *The Point with Greta Van Susteren.* A Georgetown-educated lawyer with a no-nonsense, sometimes harsh on-air style, Van Susteren had become a household name while providing legal analysis during the O. J. Simpson murder trial in 1994–95. She cohosted a talk show, *Burden of Proof,* that typically examined the criminal trial du jour. CNN attempted to broaden her appeal in 2000 with *The Point,* which offered inside-the-Beltway analysis of the day's top headlines.

But Van Susteren soon began to get the idea that the new bosses at CNN—and their bosses at AOL Time Warner—were not completely behind either her or the show. She complained that the company was spending millions to build state-of-the-art sets for new anchors in New York, while she had to settle for makeshift backdrops. Her set for *The Point,* she says, "must have cost, I don't know, fifteen hundred bucks. It had a bunch of 'Gretas' on it."

Now Van Susteren walked into her studio and found that a guest for a different show on Headline News, CNN's sister network, was sitting in her chair, waiting to be called for an appearance. This discovery did little to promote warmer relations between Van Susteren and CNN's management.

"I go back in the control room. I said, 'That's it,'" she says. "'When the show starts, I gotta have a chair to sit in front of a camera . . . that's the bare minimum.'"

That was just the beginning. During the fall and winter of 2001–02, CNN and Fox became locked in talent wars over Van Susteren and Paula Zahn, who hosted Fox's daily news show *The Edge.* The conflict included public insults and accusations, bitter litigation, and a high-profile firing. On one level, the war offered the most dramatic proof that CNN and Fox were locked in a fight for number one, but on another level it showed that cable news—once the proving ground for unknowns who might or might not become future stars—had grown entangled in the same costly star system that bedeviled the broadcast network news divisions.

Television journalists were not always treated like stars, largely because in the early days, news itself was a bit player.

One of the first regular news programs on network television was NBC's *Meet the Press,* which debuted on November 6, 1947. While *Meet the Press* grew in stature over time—to this day it holds the record as network TV's longest-running program—it was hardly considered a star-making vehicle. The original host, Lawrence Spivak, saw the weekly public affairs show largely as a promotional opportunity for his day job as editor of the *American Mercury* magazine.

NBC introduced the first nightly newscast the following year when an estimated 350,000 television sets were in use in the United States (up from 44,000 in 1947). *Camel Newsreel Theatre,* sponsored by Reynolds Tobacco, maker of Camel cigarettes, lasted all of ten minutes and consisted of host John Cameron Swayze introducing Movietone newsreels, which at the time were typically played in theaters before films started. NBC later renamed the program *Camel News Caravan* and expanded it to fifteen minutes.

But network news and news personalities really came of age in 1956 when NBC replaced Swayze with the anchor team of David Brinkley and Chet Huntley. The pair became perhaps the first stars created especially for TV news. As *The New York Times* noted, "The chemistry between the two, thanks largely to the controlled astringency of Mr. Brinkley's commentary, gave the broadcast a dominant place in the ratings." Huntley-Brinkley coverage of the 1964 Democratic convention commanded an astonishing 84 percent share of total viewers. Their closing tag lines—"Good night, Chet," "Good night, David"—became a national catchphrase.

By the 1970s, as the battle for ratings heated up, network anchors were commanding seven-figure salaries, along with mind-boggling perks. In 1976—in a groundbreaking move for sexual equality—ABC gave Barbara Walters, a former "Today Girl" on NBC's morning show, a $1 million salary to coanchor an ill-fated evening newscast with Harry Reasoner. ABC News executive Roone Arledge recalled his shock upon reading Walters's contract, which allowed virtually no ambiguity about her status: "Perusing its one-hundred-plus pages, I noted that among the perks her William Morris agents had extracted were a second secretary, a personal research assistant, a makeup consultant, a wardrobe mistress, and a hairstylist. . . . The contract stipulated that airtime and assignments were to be split down the middle with Harry, dead even, and that she'd be given equal prominence—down to the type size of her name—in all promotional campaigns."

This kind of network coddling gave Ted Turner an opportunity when he launched CNN in 1980. His fledgling cable outfit could ditch the high-priced talent and the bloated cost structure that went along with it. Upon launch, CNN's highest-paid editorial employee was George Watson, a former ABC News Washington bureau chief who signed on for $100,000 a year. Most employees had more in common with the nearly one hundred journalism grad students that CNN hired as "veejays"—greenhorn producers who would do everything, from writing copy to nuts-and-bolts camera and sound work. The pay was $3.50 an hour. As one executive explained at the time, "We have less than sixty days to turn those people into broadcast professionals."

Turner bragged about his cheap ways. At a White House dinner during the early 1980s, the Georgia mogul happened to find himself standing beside Arledge at the men's room urinals. Never one to miss the moment, Turner drawled, "I'm going to kill you network guys. I'm going to hire college kids and you're going to pay grown-ups, and I'm going to kill you."

CNN's success eventually spurred the big networks to cut editorial costs drastically. But the new rules did not apply to the big names. By 1999, the three major broadcast networks were paying their news anchors salaries usually associated with top Hollywood stars. ABC paid Peter Jennings $9 million a year, according to *Brill's Content,* while CBS's Dan Rather and NBC's Tom Brokaw each earned about $7 million. Ted Koppel of *Nightline* fame drew $8 million annually. ABC's Diane Sawyer netted $7 million.

Meanwhile, the increased competition in cable news began to push salaries higher there as well. By 1999, CNN paid Larry King $7 million a year; the roving foreign correspondent Christiane Amanpour, $2 million. MSNBC's Brian Williams, heir apparent to Tom Brokaw, made $2 million. And Fox News's Bill O'Reilly, who started at the network at less than $1 million, would soar to at least $6 million annually by 2003.

A key force behind many of these pricey deals was a bald, fast-talking man named Richard Leibner.

In August 2001, Leibner—one of the best-known TV agents in the country—called up Roger Ailes. He wanted to talk about a new contract for his client Paula Zahn. A veteran of CBS's ratings-plagued morning show, Zahn had joined Fox in 1999 as host of its evening news program, and more recently hosted a prime-time show, *The Edge with Paula Zahn.*

Leibner, an aggressive agent who is as self-promoting as he is persistent, and his New York–based N. S. Bienstock Agency have a long and colorful history of battles with network executives. A self-described "good b.s. artist," Leibner has at one time or another represented such newspersons as Diane Sawyer, Mike Wallace, Morley Safer, and Maria Shriver. He was widely credited for engineering the 1980 coup that installed his longtime client Dan Rather, then a reporter on *60 Minutes,* as the successor to Walter Cronkite on *CBS Evening News* for a then-record salary of $2.2 million per year. Leibner grew famous for wheedling huge pay packages for his top clients, which he then boasted about in the press. Behind the scenes, some executives complained bitterly that in addition to his grandstanding, Leibner wielded too much power over news divisions—or, more accurately, was draining editorial budgets on behalf of his clients. In 1983, Edward Joyce, then the president of CBS News, attacked Leibner in an angry interview with the trade paper *Variety.* "I am determined not to let the flesh peddlers affect the caliber of our broadcasts," Joyce said. The executive referred to Bienstock as "the General Motors of agents," which was meant not as flattery but to emphasize the unprecedented clout exercised by Leibner.

The *Variety* story only increased Leibner's notoriety. Bienstock continued to sign high-profile talent; in fact, Leibner's wife and longtime business partner, Carole Cooper, represents Fox News's number one star, Bill O'Reilly.

Ailes knew Leibner's reputation but was nonplussed by his call about Zahn. Her contract was up at the end of February 2002, and Ailes believed he had until the first of the year to make a decision about renewal. On the other hand, there might not be any harm in tossing out a few numbers as part of an informal preliminary negotiation. Zahn was at the time making $650,000 a year, a substantial sum but significantly less than that paid to some anchors in top local markets. Ailes said the network could perhaps offer a three-year deal that would top out at $900,000 in the final year. Ailes noted, though, that *The Edge* was not doing as well in prime time as *The O'Reilly Factor* and *Hannity and Colmes.* If Zahn's ratings did not improve, he warned Leibner, the network might be looking at a less desirable weekend slot for her. This was a bit of cage-rattling on Ailes's part: Fox wanted to keep Zahn around, at least partly because she provided a kind of political fig leaf. Zahn was a solid news veteran with no identifiable partisan background. When critics argued that Fox was right-wing talk radio transplanted to TV, the network could always point to apolitical professionals like Zahn and reaffirm its credentials as a "fair and balanced" news network.

What Ailes did not know is that Zahn had grown increasingly unhappy with the journalistic environment at Fox. She felt hard news was getting shoved aside in favor of commentators like O'Reilly and Hannity. "She thought that her career would be ruined if she got tainted as a Fox person," one executive says. "She was worried about what Fox was doing to her career. . . . Her agent was making it clear that her contract was up and she was open to offers."

A week passed, and Ailes heard nothing from Leibner. He left a message but never heard back. A few days later, on August 28, Ailes again called the agent. This time Leibner took the call. "You'll be getting a counterproposal in five minutes," he said.

Leibner faxed over a letter addressed to Ailes from Zahn. "I have received an offer from CNN . . . for my services following the end of the term of my current employment with Fox," the letter began. Attached was a copy of the CNN offer, which was worth $2 million a year. Fox was given just five business days to match the offer or Zahn would leave. She ended the letter on a conciliatory note. She recalled that in an earlier conversation, Ailes had promised that they would remain friends no matter what happened with the contract talks. "I cannot tell you how important that is to me on a personal level," Zahn wrote.

Ailes's surprise turned to anger. While Leibner and Zahn's tactics were hardly unheard of in the TV business, Ailes took them personally. "We had taken her off the scrap heap," one Fox executive says, alluding to her prior experience on the low-rated *CBS Early Show.* "She was damaged goods at CBS. . . . One thing Roger can't stand is disloyalty."

Ailes, by this point in a rage, called a meeting of his top executives. Between profane outbursts, he explained the situation and asked for advice. He was not about to pay Zahn anything close to what Leibner said CNN was offering—not after she went behind his back this way. Even worse was the idea of CNN doing a victory dance in the media after poaching one of Fox's prime-time stars. That was the kind of thing that could steal momentum from Fox just when it looked ready to overtake its rival in the ratings.

As the executives absorbed all this, Brian Lewis, Fox News's top media relations executive, piped up. "Why don't we fire her?" he asked.

Silence fell on the room. Dianne Brandi, Fox News's vice president of legal affairs, nodded. "Yeah, we can do that," she said.

On August 30—two days after Zahn's agent notified Fox of CNN's $2 million offer—Ailes received a two-page typewritten handout from Lewis. The memo spelled out the network's various options in dealing with the wayward newswoman, along with pros and cons. Fox could essentially allow Zahn to leave and issue a joint press release with CNN simply saying that she was switching networks. This was the "nice guy approach," as Lewis put it. But "unless we word [the release] strongly and kill her on background [that is, in off-the-record conversations with reporters], CNN would appear to be the victor." As alternatives, Fox could do nothing or remove Zahn later as her contract wound down, but those options gave the network little control of the situation, Lewis wrote.

The last option was to fire her for cause—arguing that by secretly negotiating with CNN, Zahn had breached her contract. Lewis wrote that this move "looks sincere" and "sends [a] message thru [the] ranks and to [the] industry" that betrayal would not be tolerated. Referring to Fox's underdog status, Lewis added that an "outnumbered army must have surprise on its side." The risks were that Zahn might be turned into a "martyr" and end up bad-mouthing her former employer.

Lewis's memo in hand, Ailes fretted about the situation that weekend. He called Lewis at home several times, repeating, "I can't look like a bully."

On the afternoon of September 4, Ailes called Zahn into his office. He never mentioned that the network was weighing whether to sack her.

"I just want to look you in the eye and ask what you're doing," Ailes said.

Zahn was polite if not warm. "You'll have to speak to my agent," she said.

The next morning around eleven, Ailes cruised down the hall into Lewis's office and sank into a chair. He was clearly agitated. "I hope you're right about this," he said to Lewis. "You know, the Japanese bombed Pearl Harbor, and they ended up losing. Isaacson controls a lot of the press. They all love him."

An hour later Zahn arrived for work. At 2:28, Brandi, the legal affairs executive, went upstairs to the anchor's office and told her she was fired. Zahn was somewhat surprised at the peremptory move but took the news in stride. Two minutes later, Fox blasted word of Zahn's termination over AP Express, a news release service that goes to many of the country's major media organizations. Soon Fox was swamped with calls from reporters.

Lewis anticipated no problems as long as Ailes could check his impulses and stick to the script when speaking with the media. As Fox saw it, Zahn was a disloyal employee, and her ratings were nothing to write home about. Lewis left early that day to teach a night class at a college in New Jersey. In the middle of the class, he went out in the hall to answer his cell phone. A young associate in the Fox publicity office said it was urgent. "Roger just called Paula a dead raccoon," he said.

In a conversation late in the day with *The New York Times*'s Bill Carter, probably the nation's most powerful TV reporter, Ailes turned aside the suggestion that Zahn's ratings had in fact grown. "I could have put a dead raccoon on the air this year and gotten a better rating than last year," he said. "All our shows are up."

Lewis cringed. While the content of the quote was essentially the Fox spin, Ailes had put his own unforgettable polish on it. He sure had a funny way of protecting himself from looking like a bully. "We just lost the spin on this because of that quote," Lewis thought to himself.

Carter's story the next day included the "dead raccoon" quote, albeit buried in the fourteenth paragraph. Nevertheless, the turn of phrase was memorable enough. The remark summed up the increasing vitriol that marked the cable news battle; the Associated Press later called Ailes's insult "legendary."

Fox was still not done with l'affaire Zahn. The same day word of her ouster spread, Fox filed suit against Leibner and Bienstock alleging "intentional interference" with Zahn's contract. Fox argued that the anchor's contract gave Fox the right to match any offer for up to three months after the end of her deal. While the New York State Supreme Court tossed out the suit in March 2002, Ailes had once again sent a strong message that opponents crossed him at their peril.

Zahn, meanwhile, was already receiving a warm welcome from her new bosses at CNN. On September 6, the same day *The New York Times* story ran, Zahn told reporters at a news conference, "I am so excited about what lies ahead here at CNN." She was slotted for a three-hour morning show from a brand-new multimillion-dollar studio on the ground floor of the Time-Life Building in New York.

The studio idea came from Jamie Kellner, the chief of Turner Broadcasting. As he remembers it, "I was walking by the Time-Life Building one day, and I saw that front place [the ground floor facing the street] was empty. They were going to use it for a *People* magazine museum or something like that. And I called over to the corporate guys and said, 'Who owns this space?' It was the perfect place to put a studio."

It also afforded Ailes the perfect opportunity for yet another swipe at his former anchor. After the studio was built, trucks advertising Fox News channel could be seen driving up and down Sixth Avenue, clearly in the range of CNN's cameras.

As CNN hailed its latest star, another was halfway out the door.

In addition to her problems with chairs and sets, Van Susteren was, like many of her colleagues, deeply angered by the AOL–Time Warner merger. She felt that bosses at the online giant had rushed to throw their weight around at CNN. Many of her friends at the network—reporters such as Roger Cossack and Joie Chen, as well as executives such as general counsel Eve Burton—had been either laid off or soon would be in cost-cutting maneuvers. "I thought it was despicable, and I also thought that they destroyed the product we were trying to put on the air; and the way that they were destroying morale was unbelievable," she says. "You'd walk down halls, and there'd be missing name tags every day."

In November, not long after the chair incident, Van Susteren sent an email to Jamie Kellner, reminding him that her contract was due to expire in March 2002. "The place was so disorganized that I wanted to know what their intention was for CNN," she says. "He sent an email back to me which essentially was 'I'm too busy. Talk to somebody else.'"

Van Susteren's disdain was returned by her bosses in Atlanta. Many CNN executives disliked her focus on crime stories, which they felt were too tabloid for a classy network. They also found her on-camera style abrasive and singled out her voice for special criticism, with "grating" the adjective of choice in the executive suite. While none of the male executives wanted to be viewed as sexist, one gets the sense that Van Susteren—with her unfashionably styled dirt-brown hair, angular features, and downturned mouth—compared unfavorably in their eyes to the sexy blondes who increasingly turned up reading the news.

"She's not, um, Paula Zahn," one former CNN executive says of Van Susteren.

The sales team in New York reported that major advertisers didn't like Van Susteren, either. Blue-chip companies steered clear of *The Point* because of its relentless focus on crime, they said. By comparison, *Moneyline with Lou Dobbs* scored much lower ratings than *The Point,* partly because of *Moneyline*'s earlier time slot, but made far more profit because companies such as Fidelity Investments felt it was important to be on Dobbs's program.

"Greta was controversial," the former executive says. "The purists at CNN just couldn't abide [her show]. She was brash, opinionated. There are people who felt she was low-rent . . . you know, the Jim Waltons, the Eason Jordans. Quite a few purists just really didn't like her."

Meanwhile, a smaller group of CNN insiders felt that Van Susteren was smart and worked hard, and she was by now a recognizable brand name on the network. That should count for something. Some effort should be made to keep her.

Thrown into the middle of all this was Walter Isaacson, who saw merit in both sides of the Greta debate. "Which is why," he says with irony, "I was a bad TV executive."

Over Thanksgiving, CNN executive Sid Bedingfield called Van Susteren in Paris, where she was vacationing. He said the network had decided to pull her show in favor of an hour-long broadcast from Christiane Amanpour, who was reporting from the war in Afghanistan.

"This made no sense to me," Van Susteren says. "I was doing breaking news. I was doing investigative pieces." Besides that, her show was CNN's number 2–rated broadcast in prime time, after *Larry King Live.* When she protested the move, Bedingfield promised she could have a half hour back in prime time upon her return.

The bosses in Atlanta felt that Van Susteren was angling for a guaranteed slot in prime time during her upcoming contract negotiations. "Greta was looking for a longer-term commitment than the network was willing to make," Kellner says. "And there just wasn't a strong sense at CNN that they saw a long-term place for her. . . . It wasn't me trying to get rid of her."

Van Susteren's contract had a provision that barred her from negotiating for jobs with rival companies for ninety days prior to the expiration of her contract. That gave her until the end of December to scout offers.

Van Susteren, who months before had flirted with the notion of joining NBC News, quickly determined her next move. "I went in, sat down, talked with Roger," she says, "and I think Roger thought—this is my guess—there's probably a little piece of him that thought I wouldn't leave CNN, and I was playing the game of trying to run up the number, playing one group after another. You know, you try to get a bidding war on yourself."

But she was serious about leaving—so serious that she even told her bosses at CNN that she was meeting with Fox. And when an offer materialized days later for a show on Fox's prime-time lineup, Van Susteren related that as well. Under her contract, CNN had the right to match any offers. "Suddenly, they were willing to give me the moon," Van Susteren says. "They were talking about how I was a CNN brand, and they were saying how bad Fox was and how I'd never like it at Fox."

Isaacson flew up from Atlanta in December to try to mend fences. He met Van Susteren late one afternoon at the Ritz Carlton in Washington's West End. While the host sipped a cup of coffee, Isaacson spelled out the reasons he felt she should stay at CNN. Whenever she had wanted something, he said, the network had delivered it to her.

"When you needed a chair, I got it for you," Isaacson said.

Van Susteren laughed. "To tell you the truth, Walter, I think when the show starts, you ought to have some place to put your anchor, just some place."

Almost as soon as the words left his mouth, Isaacson realized that bringing up the chair was probably not the best tactic. "Can I take that off the table?" he asked half-jokingly.

But the Isaacson charm, so effective on reporters at *Time* magazine, was clearly not working this time. When the two parted at the Ritz, Isaacson told Van Susteren it looked as if she'd made up her mind to leave CNN.

"Walter, I told you, no commitments," she replied.

Van Susteren was making $800,000 a year as host of *The Point*. CNN offered to bump her up to $900,000. Fox's offer was only $800,000, but Van Susteren had insisted all along that money was not the primary consideration behind her decision.

On December 31, Van Susteren officially notified CNN that she was headed for Fox, but some at the network had trouble letting go. Several days later, Van Susteren says, she received "a bazillion phone calls from all the women at CNN," including anchor Judy Woodruff and producer Eileen O'Connor, expressing concern about her situation and inviting her to call back to talk things over. Van Susteren believes the phone calls were orchestrated by CNN executives who worried that her departure might renew criticism that the network was slow to promote women. Six months earlier Van Susteren had joined a group of women who complained to management after Eve Burton, the general counsel, had been laid off. Now, with a prominent female host leaving, "they thought, 'Oh, my God, now we might have another woman problem.'"

If so, the problem was going away. Van Susteren's husband and lawyer, John Coale, sent CNN a letter saying that she was headed to Fox as a "wake-up call" to executives "so that CNN will re-evaluate its new environment before it's too late." Coale wrote that the network had traditionally stiffed women and minorities, and had made little effort to promote *The Point.* And since the merger with AOL, he added, journalism was taking a backseat to ratings and profits.

"Greta just can't watch anymore," Coale wrote.

14

War and Ratings

"We were just ahead of ourselves at that time." —NBC's Bob Wright on the America's Talking network

For the first few years of its existence, Fox News played the scrappy underdog to CNN. But by late January 2002, that role was no longer viable. At a senior management meeting, Roger Ailes felt compelled to warn his staff against overconfidence.

Earlier that month, Fox News had for the first time beat CNN in total viewership during both prime time and throughout the day. The ratings landscape had shifted dramatically following the terrorist attacks the previous September. While CNN's averages had been slowly drifting downward since at least early 2000, the network had gone into the attacks maintaining a slight edge over Fox. When the World Trade Center was destroyed, CNN's numbers spiraled to record heights as viewers sought breaking news of the tragedy. Ratings for Fox and MSNBC spiked as well, although not by quite as much. Over the summer, Fox staffers had noticed internally that they were within striking distance of CNN, but the terror attacks disrupted the network's momentum. As the war on terror progressed through the fall, however, something extraordinary happened. Viewership for CNN eroded to levels generally seen during less cataclysmic breaking stories, such as the death of Princess Diana in 1997 or the Columbine school shootings in 1999. Fox's numbers, on the other hand, stayed robust, much more so than they were just prior to September 11. Charted on a graph, the numbers for CNN from fall 2001 resemble a stalagmite—steep climb, sharp point, sheer drop. Fox's stats are more like a mountain range rising from the foothills. In January 2002, the two lines intersected as CNN tumbled below its rival. MSNBC remained mired in distant third. In prime time during January, Fox averaged 1.1 million viewers, trailed by CNN (921,000) and MSNBC (358,000). For the entire day, Fox enjoyed a more than 10 percent advantage over CNN even though CNN, with 86 million subscribers, was available in 12 percent more homes than Fox.

There are two possible explanations for the sudden Fox surge. One is that the terror attacks may have simply galvanized Fox viewers to watch longer, which hiked numbers for the network's entire lineup. What seems at least as likely, though, is that the tumultuous events of that autumn led audiences to sample all the cable news networks. Viewers who had previously seldom watched Fox grew to like not just the network's fast-paced newscasts but also its unabashed pro-American orientation. If terrorism had made Americans feel wounded, frightened, and confused, Fox helped wash those feelings away, becoming a beacon of moral certainty and defiance. Even more than the 2000 election, the terrorist attacks, or more accurately their aftermath, were to Fox News what Gulf War I had been to CNN: the defining news event that put the network on the map. If viewers during Desert Storm wanted just the facts, viewers post–September 11 wanted a rallying point. To paraphrase NBC's Bob Wright, Roger Ailes had converted viewers to his church.

Ailes reminded reporters that Murdoch's cable news quest had been dismissed as folly not even five years earlier. "He said that there's room and we can win, and nobody believed him," Ailes told the Associated Press.

In an executive meeting shortly afterward, Ailes boasted that never before in the history of cable TV had an upstart network toppled an established brand. MTV, ESPN, and Lifetime had all withstood challenges and remained on top of their respective categories. Yet Ailes didn't want anyone to feel complacent. He noted that despite its success, Fox News was still just the twelfth highest-rated cable network. "Our goal," he said, "should be to be number one."

CNN responded to the Fox victory by pointing to its own ratings gains and, at least implicitly, attacking Fox's approach to the news. "Fox and CNN do different things," a CNN spokeswoman said. "If you watch CNN, we have a full day of smart, hard newscasts that cover the world and break news daily."

Greta Van Susteren was not the last CNN personality poached by Fox News.

In the wake of September 11, as it became clear the United States faced lengthy military actions in the Middle East, Fox News recognized that its competitor remained far better situated to cover continuing international stories. Fox News's John Moody was especially puzzled about how to staff Afghanistan, where the United States was embarking on a war against the ruling Taliban. Moody knew of only one Western reporter permanently based in the country, the AP's Kathy Gannon. News organizations that wished to send reporters to Afghanistan faced a complicated process of sending staffers to Pakistan for visas and then waiting for permission from the Taliban, which was at best an uncertain process.

"It was one of the few times in my career when I was really ready to throw up my hands and just say, 'Roger, we cannot do this,'" Moody recalls.

But then Moody became aware of a veteran CNN reporter, Steve Harrigan, who had recently been dispatched to a tiny northern area of

Afghanistan controlled by anti-Taliban forces. Harrigan was usually based in the Moscow bureau and had distinguished himself with some intrepid coverage of the Russian war in Chechnya. Moody tracked down Harrigan's agent, Steve Herz, and learned that CNN had let the reporter's contract lapse. Harrigan was being paid on a month-to-month basis. Herz arranged a three-way call with Moody in New York and Harrigan on his satellite phone. Harrigan, it turned out, was very receptive to switching networks and within a few days had agreed to join Fox News.

Harrigan explained to his puzzled entourage of Afghan guides and translators that they would no longer be working for CNN. Most of them had never heard of Fox News, which unlike CNN has almost nonexistent distribution overseas. Through operatives in Uzbekistan, Fox News smuggled a video phone to Harrigan, which allowed him to file live reports as the United States began its push against the Taliban.

Within an hour or so of filing his first Fox dispatch, Harrigan heard his satellite phone ring. It was Walter Isaacson calling from Atlanta, hoping to renew Harrigan's CNN deal. The reporter apologized and said it was too late.

Phil Donahue, the white-haired veteran of the talk-show wars, gazed into the camera and announced, "We are, all of us, pumped."

Donahue, returning to television after a six-year retirement, was premiering his own new show on MSNBC opposite CNN's *Connie Chung Tonight* and *The O'Reilly Factor.* Network executives believed they had found a magic bullet. Donahue had pioneered the confessional daytime talk show, producing nearly seven thousand syndicated hours starting in 1967. In his mid-'70s prime, the white-haired host ruled the daytime airwaves with a mix of homey reassurance and distilled feminism. Pre-Oprah, the earnest and nonthreatening Donahue gave his core female audience a low-grade dose of empowerment. *Donahue* had an unmistakable liberal bent; frequent guests included Jesse Jackson, Ralph Nader, and Gloria Steinem. Starting in the late 1980s, though, competition from Geraldo Rivera, Ricki Lake, and others forced *Donahue* away from popular political issues and self-improvement and into seamier topics; the show may have hit a low point with such themes as "Dressing Up Like a Baby for Sexual Pleasure." The program began to seem strained and outmoded. *Donahue* finally signed off in 1996, whereupon the host sailed off in his fifty-six-foot boat for a retirement full of pleasure trips to Key West and the Bahamas.

But the changing cable news landscape led NBC executives to believe that twenty-first-century America might be ready for a second helping of the sixty-six-year-old Donahue. The network was already familiar with the host; at one point toward the end of its run *Donahue* was produced at a studio in 30 Rock. NBC, moreover, was beginning to realize that Fox News's success was no fluke; viewers were obviously gravitating toward punditry and analysis. If Fox had already commandeered right-leaning audiences with voices like Bill O'Reilly's and Sean Hannity's, then perhaps MSNBC could make inroads with a liberal voice like Phil Donahue's.

At a May 2002 event celebrating NBC's seventy-fifth anniversary, Bob Wright told listeners that the impeachment of President Clinton had spurred "the biggest change in television news" in the past twenty years. "Cable news is now opinion news," Wright said. "People want to see a debate." He added that America's Talking, the NBC cable channel once headed by Roger Ailes, could be seen as a precursor to Fox News.

MSNBC president and general manager Erik Sorenson would oversee the strategic shift. As Wright admitted in a later interview, "The cable news business has changed a lot in the past two years, and we have to kind of reorient ourselves to that change."

MSNBC hired Jerry Nachman, the combative former editor of the *New York Post,* to help lead the charge into opinion journalism. Nachman would host his own freewheeling hour as a lead-in to Donahue's 8 P.M. show. *Donahue,* at least theoretically, would attract those left-leaning viewers who were turned off by *The O'Reilly Factor* on Fox.

One casualty of the new lineup was *The News with Brian Williams,* which had been a mainstay of MSNBC since the channel went on the air. Williams's straightforward newscast aired in early prime time on MSNBC and was then rebroadcast on CNBC, where the audience was typically larger. But the anchor was unhappy as MSNBC drifted to opinion, and he asked that his program air only on CNBC. "I started feeling like the attractive Munster daughter," Williams says. "I said, 'You know, it's very apparent that we stick out like a sore thumb in the prime time [MSNBC] schedule.' . . . I had to get off." NBC News chief Neil Shapiro had arrived at the same conclusion independently, and *The News* was taken off MSNBC in the summer of 2002 to make way for *Donahue.* To some insiders the move had symbolic importance. The nightly newscast with Tom Brokaw's anointed successor could no longer be seen on the NBC cable channel ostensibly devoted to twenty-four-hour news.

Donahue premiered on MSNBC on July 15. The host may have been pumped, but viewers did not reciprocate the feeling. His show settled into a predictable right-left cross talk (the premiere featured a less than stirring debate with conservative firebrand Pat Buchanan over the separation between church and state). Two weeks into the launch, *Donahue* averaged 620,000 total viewers, trailing CNN's *Connie Chung Tonight* (746,000) and Fox's *O'Reilly Factor* (2 million). By early September, Donahue was speculating on the air that the network would soon ax his show. "If we don't make noise in six months, it's going to be hard for me to tell my family that I was treated unfairly," he said. When the program was finally canceled not quite six months later, Donahue complained that the network acted too soon.

Some within NBC believed that *Donahue* proved the company had lost its way in trying to turn around MSNBC. One former NBC executive pointed out that Donahue had hosted a CNBC show in the early 1990s that did poorly in the ratings. "And that was when he was known and a hot commodity," this former executive says.

One person with his own distinctive take on the *Donahue* disaster was Roger Ailes. "He made his name convincing all the women in America that their husbands were fucking their secretaries," Ailes says of the erstwhile talk king. "Now all those women are sixty-five or seventy, and they want their husband to go *anywhere.* They don't care who he's fucking. They didn't want [Donahue] on nuclear nonproliferation. They didn't give a shit."

In March 2002, just weeks after Fox News's historic ratings victory, Walter Isaacson hosted an enormous off-site management retreat at his loft in Atlanta. More than a hundred CNN executives and producers showed up for a fateful discussion of the network's future.

By this time, the management at CNN Center realized that MSNBC was going to try to chase Fox with a talk-radio-style format. Rumors circulated that NBC was in preliminary negotiations with pundits like Pat Buchanan and Jesse Ventura. Isaacson was nervous. "I kind of thought Donahue was going to go off the charts and succeed," Isaacson says. "Shows how much I knew about television." Still, if the opinion strategy worked half as well for MSNBC as it had for Fox, CNN could find itself in deep trouble. CNN needed to decide if it should try opinion as well or stick with its plan to update Ted Turner's old "news is the star" motto.

The retreat was "sort of a day and a half of discussions [culminating] with a full day of 'Okay, what are we really going to do?'" Isaacson says.

He compared the choices facing CNN to a pilot's fail-safe points during takeoff. Would the network proceed with a news-oriented strategy or abort that maneuver and try to outfox Fox?

To Isaacson there was never any doubt about which direction CNN should choose. He just wanted to see a show of hands from Eason Jordan, Teya Ryan, Jim Walton, and his other lieutenants. "I knew if I gathered everybody there which way they'd want to go," he says. "Everybody basically [wanted] to stick with what CNN was built to do."

When Jamie Kellner dropped by the loft, Isaacson pulled him aside. He told the TBS boss that the group had decided CNN would do shows that are "basically newsier" than the prime-time shows on Fox and MSNBC. Isaacson was worried Kellner would argue that in the heated cable competition, a continued emphasis on hard news would be costly and generate relatively low ratings.

Instead, Kellner endorsed the news approach. "I get it," Kellner told Isaacson. "It's a good way to go because, first of all, [news] is what you're all about. It is your brand. It's hard to go against brand. Secondly, MS is going to go the other route. And that's good for you because you will be more distinctive."

The issue was settled. CNN had bright new graphics, stronger promotion, and fresh prime-time hosts such as Connie Chung and Aaron Brown. But it would still stick to Turner's original plan. News was and would remain the star.

MSNBC's ratings woes were just one of the myriad problems afflicting the executive suite at 30 Rock. Corporate warfare estranged Bob Wright from not just NBC News chief Andy Lack but also his onetime GE mentor Jack Welch.

In May 2001, NBC announced that Lack would be named president and chief operating officer of the network. He would replace Wright, who was kicked upstairs to chairman and CEO and also earned a vice chairman title at GE. Although Wright was still the nominal boss at 30 Rock, Lack would have day-to-day control and was widely assumed to be Wright's heir apparent. Publicly, Wright seemed ready to hand over the reins, telling reporters that he and Lack would be more comfortable running NBC together.

But privately Wright—perhaps goaded by his wife, Suzanne, the ambitious "First Lady of NBC" whom some insiders compared to Nancy Reagan—decided he was not ready to take a backseat. Wright countermanded Lack's decisions, which predictably led to tensions. "There were some awkward moments with Bob," Lack later told *The Washington Post.* "He wanted to spend more time at NBC, and that created certain problems. I thought I'd have a little more running room than I did."

Wright's relationship with Welch was crumbling as well. By all accounts the two men had essentially stopped speaking around the time Welch retired as GE chairman in the fall of 2001. Several NBC insiders say that Wright, a devout Catholic, was offended by Welch's highly publicized affair with Suzy Wetlaufer, the attractive and socially adventurous editor of the *Harvard Business Review.* News of their extramarital dalliance, splashed across the pages of *The Wall Street Journal,* led to an acrimonious divorce between Welch and his second wife, Jane.

Wright may well have been repelled by the Wetlaufer mess, but as NBC boss he has maintained warm relations with many executives and celebrities who have private lives at least as scandalous as Welch's. One former NBC executive offers a more plausible explanation for Wright's alienation, saying that the NBC chairman blamed Welch for engineering the switch that handed the network presidency to Lack. After decades of working in Welch's shadow, Wright may have felt that his retirement-bound mentor had undermined him and deliberately tried to hasten the end of the Wright regime at 30 Rock. Throughout his career "Bob did everything Jack asked," the former executive says. "It was Jack [who] had the final call, and Bob kind of bridled under that, I think." A *New York Times* story in April 2002 reported that Wright had tried unsuccessfully to persuade Welch's successor at GE, Jeffrey Immelt, to remove Lack.

Given his growing rift with Lack, Wright may have had little incentive to try to rescue MSNBC from the ratings mire. Lack, after all, had direct oversight of the cable news network during his NBC tenure. "I think Bob had interests in making MSNBC not look good so Andy didn't look good," the former executive says.

In January 2003, Lack was lured away from NBC by his old friend and former boss Sir Howard Stringer, the former chief of CBS News, to run Sony Music Entertainment. Wright quickly moved to consolidate his power. He announced that NBC would not be naming a replacement for the president's job and that the executives who had formerly reported to Lack would now report directly to Wright.

Fox News's success in the ratings, not surprisingly, boosted its bottom line. In 2001, the network for the first time finished the year with positive cash flow. Fox earned roughly $20 million on total net revenue of $208 million, according to figures from Kagan World Media. That compared to negative cash flow of nearly $30 million the previous year.

By the end of 2002, cable operators paid Fox News an average of seventeen cents per subscriber each month. While CNN and Headline News were still far ahead with about thirty-seven cents per subscriber, Fox had made enormous strides since 1996, when Rupert Murdoch had to pay cable operators to launch the service. Despite NBC's considerable leverage with its broadcast network and other cable channels, MSNBC was earning only thirteen cents per subscriber. And while NBC preferred to lump the channel's results with the rest of NBC News, MSNBC by itself did not return an annual profit for the first six years of its existence.

"If you're a big company and you want to buy a spot on *Friends,* you also have to buy on [NBC-owned] Telemundo, CNBC, and MS," says a highly placed source at NBC News. "That's why they keep making their margin. [MSNBC] would be shuttered by now if it weren't for the [advertising] sales agreements."

Even before he finished speaking, Jamie Kellner realized the crowd was not on his side. It was December 2002, and the Turner Broadcasting chief had just pitched the AOL Time Warner board on a potential merger between ABC News and CNN. For years executives at ABC and CBS had toyed with the idea of merging their news divisions with the cable network, but talks had always faltered over cost and control issues. Now some reversals at ABC's parent, Walt Disney Company, had made executives there more receptive to a deal. The network had suffered catastrophic ratings during the 2001–02 season, largely the result of a sudden decline in the game show *Who Wants to Be a Millionaire?* Due in part to a large stable of such high-priced stars as Ted Koppel, Peter Jennings, Diane Sawyer, and Barbara Walters, ABC News was essentially a break-even operation. Some reports indicated that the division made a profit of only $30 million a year, or about one-tenth of the estimated sum earned by NBC News. If ABC could find a well-heeled partner to share news gathering costs, a great deal of pressure could be removed from the network's balance sheet.

Kellner believed a merger could make sense for CNN as well. "I don't see twenty-four-hour news as a business that's going to grow a lot in the future, because you have now a lot of competition," he says. "So the way you increase your profitability in a business like that is to find ways to lower your costs." CNN would also get immediate access to marquee talent such as Jennings; during a major breaking story, the anchor could finish up *World News Tonight* and then switch over to CNN and offer several more hours of (hopefully high-rated) coverage.

During the fall, Kellner and his boss, AOL Time Warner's Jeff Bewkes, met with ABC and Disney executives to discuss ways the merger might work. People familiar with the proposed deal said that while CNN would have clear financial and editorial control, ABC News chief David Westin would be given a major operational role if not outright oversight of the combined entity. At the end of the board meeting, Kellner gave the directors a brief handout summarizing the proposal and highlighted the selling points. Among them: CNN would save $500 million in operational costs after the merger.

But one of the directors had done his own spadework prior to the meeting: Ted Turner. The vice chairman of AOL Time Warner had initially supported the idea of combining with ABC News, but the more he thought about it, the less he liked the deal. He expressed his reservations to other directors the weekend prior to the meeting. "By the time he got to New York, he had gotten [to] a bunch of the board members and [said], 'Guess what [these] crazy guys want to do now,'" one TBS executive says.

Kellner had no sooner finished his presentation than Turner went on the attack. ABC News was hardly worth anything, the cable mogul told the other directors, and broadcast news operations were destined for obsolescence anyway. Why should the company take a chance by hooking up with a dying brand? What good was ABC News to CNN?

Turner and Kellner had never gotten along well, but the criticisms seemed to go beyond a mere grudge. Turner was correct in pointing out that ABC News made relatively little money. Executives might also find it difficult to combine two news organizations with very different cultures, histories, and cost structures. AOL Time Warner was already being attacked in the press and on Wall Street for failing to deliver on *its* merger promises. Since AOL swallowed Time Warner, the stock price had plummeted and CEO Jerry Levin and top lieutenant Bob Pittman had been driven from their posts. The last thing the parent company needed was another failed merger for rival media organizations to lambaste.

Then there was Turner, who still wielded enormous power as the largest individual stockholder in AOL Time Warner. Turner could make an unpleasant enemy, as Levin learned in late 2001. The CNN founder told anyone who would listen that Levin had never bothered to consult with him about the AOL merger and that Levin then added to the insult by essentially firing Turner in the new corporate structure. Indeed, since the merger Turner had made a new career out of second-guessing AOL Time Warner management decisions. Dick Parsons, Levin's diplomatic successor, seemed understandably eager to placate the aggrieved mogul. One of Parsons's first acts upon taking the helm at AOL Time Warner was to call Turner and ask him to stay with the company—as close as Turner was going to get to an apology from AOLTW.

With Parsons not eager to squander his newfound credit with Turner, Kellner's plan seemed destined for the scrap heap. Shortly after the meeting, Parsons was quoted as saying that AOLTW had "hit the pause button" on a CNN-ABC merger.

When the two ran into each other shortly after the board meeting, a miffed Kellner asked Turner why he had changed his mind about a deal with ABC. Turner replied, "This company can't afford to make mistakes."

15

"A Line in the Sand"

"There is a longstanding tradition in the mainstream press of middle-of-the-road journalism that is objective and fair. I would hate to see that fall victim to a panic about the Fox effect." —CBS News president Andrew Heyward during Gulf War II, in ***The New York Times,*** **April 16, 2003**

Eason Jordan held the phone to his ear, listening to an Iraqi official rant about CNN's coverage. It was March 2003; Gulf War II was less than three days old.

Relations between the network and Saddam Hussein's government were never warm, but tensions grew rapidly in the run-up to Gulf War II. A few months earlier the Iraqi Information Minister, Mohammed Saeed Al-Sahaf, had told Jordan that CNN journalists sent to northern Iraq would "suffer the severest possible consequences"—a threat that Jordan took to mean they would be murdered.

Now bombs were raining on Baghdad in the Pentagon's "shock and awe" campaign. American tanks rolled northward from the Kuwaiti border toward the capital. Cable news viewers saw camouflage-helmeted reporters "embedded" with military units file extensive videophone dispatches, live and unedited, even when the only action to report was a sandstorm.

CNN went into the war with some distinct advantages. It was still renowned as the network that brought Gulf War I to the world. In January, with another Saddam Hussein showdown looming, Jordan, CNN's chief news executive, told reporters, "We're very much committed to trying to own the story, as best we can, just as we did in '91." Senior management had approved the expenditure of an extra $35 million to cover the conflict, a commitment that Fox News officials privately admitted they could not match. "We certainly recognized that CNN was not dead and that it was not going to be easy to cover the same war they covered and to keep our lead," says Fox News's John Moody. CNN spent $200,000 just to buy the latest videophones for its embedded reporters.

Meanwhile, Iraqi officials booted most Western correspondents from Baghdad just before the shooting started—including those for Fox News. CNN's Nic Robertson appeared to be the city's only remaining reporter for a major American TV network. It looked as if CNN was on the verge of another dramatic wartime coup. As the bombs fell, however, CNN's luck ran out.

Al-Sahaf accused Jordan of making up news. CNN's videophone coverage, he charged, was actually shot in the California desert by Hollywood filmmakers. The network was being unfair to the Iraqi side.

"The final conversation was with a senior Information Ministry official over there, Odai al-Taie, whom I've known for many, many years," Jordan says. "He was just shouting at the top of his lungs a lot of obscenities. He said, 'CNN is worse than the U.S. military. Your people have to leave now,' and just slammed down the phone."

Jordan had mixed feelings. The network would not get the opportunity to repeat its journalistic heroics of 1991. The expulsion meant that CNN was going to miss a big chunk of the story, but at least its reporters and crew would be safe. "Safety was the big issue for us, 'cause we've experienced pain here. We lost seven people in Somalia in '93, and I'll be damned if we were gonna go through that again," Jordan says.

The next morning Robertson and his crew were on the road to Amman, Jordan.

John Moody had his own Iraq problems. After the war in Afghanistan, Fox News realized it had to maintain some sort of presence in Iraq, which President Bush had already identified in his 2002 State of the Union address as comprising an "axis of evil" with Iran and North Korea. Moody obtained a visa to visit Iraq to see if he could wangle some reporting teams into the country. Upon deplaning, he and other Americans were separated from the other passengers and ordered to submit to an AIDS test. "They show you these really bloody, wretched, rusty needles and say, 'Please roll up your sleeve,'" Moody says. Officials persisted until Moody paid $120 to forgo the test.

His visits with Iraqi bureaucrats produced many of the same complaints that CNN heard about its coverage. Hussein's advisers told Moody that Fox News was biased and pro-American, that the network was a shill for Bush and hated Iraq. Moody did not directly dispute these accusations; instead, he replied that Fox News's pro-American stance had made it a favorite among White House officials. "If you have any messages to get to the administration," he told the Iraqis, "you'd better put [them] on Fox, 'cause that's what's turned on over there nowadays."

The argument worked, at least temporarily. As Washington rumbled with war talk in mid-2002, Baghdad granted Fox News about fifteen visas, or enough for three reporting teams. Steve Harrigan was dispatched to help lead the Fox News efforts.

Meanwhile, Moody and other Fox News executives visited Washington in December for an off-the-record meeting with Defense Secretary Donald Rumsfeld. The network was leaning toward participating in the Pentagon's "embedding" program that would allow reporters to travel with military units. But Moody and others still had some concerns. One of the main reasons for embedding in the first place was to counter complaints that the Pentagon had kept reporters too far away from the action in Gulf War I. How could news organizations be sure that embedding was not merely another form of government control? It was plain, moreover, that many military commanders hated the idea of having reporters with cameras tag along with combat units. Would journalists who ran afoul of the rules end up being treated like boot-camp hazing victims? Rumsfeld assured Moody and the others that the Pentagon would not censor reporting from the field. Military commanders would remove from the scene of combat any reporters who broke the rules but would not take further punitive steps.

"What he basically said is 'We have to trust each other a little bit,'" Moody says.

Like many other news executives and reporters, Moody became over time a fan of embedding, calling it "one of the most successful radical experiments in military history." The "radical experiment" did not solve Fox News' problems in Baghdad, however. On the eve of the war, Iraq complained again of biased reporting and ejected the entire Fox staff, along with personnel from most other American networks. Fox still had live pictures of the capital, provided through exchange agreements with Arabic networks such as Al Jazeera, al-Arabia TV, and the Middle Eastern Broadcasting Company. But without a correspondent in the field, Fox appeared to be at an enormous disadvantage to CNN.

When CNN's Nic Robertson and his crew were thrown out of the country days later, Moody could scarcely contain his delight. "Whatever kind of news gods there are intervened so that we were on a level playing field with CNN," Moody says. "Once they threw Nic out, I think that's when their plan to dominate us fell apart. . . . They really didn't think that they were ever going to be denied access to Baghdad."

Another early casualty of the war was *Connie Chung Tonight.*

When the war started on March 20, the three cable news networks—as well as the four major broadcast networks—switched to wall-to-wall coverage with no commercial interruptions. In the lingo of television, this is known as "sustaining coverage" and is reserved for the very biggest news events, such as the terrorist attacks of September 11.

Chung's program, like most others, was temporarily shelved for round-the-clock war news. Her only on-air appearances were to deliver occasional updates. But after a few days, the former CBS anchor was growing restless. Fox News had brought back *The O'Reilly Factor,* and Chung believed her show, CNN's top-rated program, should also return to its slot. The Iraq war was generating a lot of news, and viewers would drift away for good if she did not soon return to the 8 P.M. hour.

Chung visited CNN Center to plead her case, but as it happened, CNN had just undergone the latest in a seemingly endless series of management shuffles. The people who had hired Chung a little more than a year earlier were now gone. In January, just days after extensively briefing TV reporters on the network's war plans and approximately eighteen months after taking the job, CNN chairman Walter Isaacson announced he was leaving to head up the Aspen Institute, a nonprofit global affairs organization. He was also preparing to publish a biography of Benjamin Franklin and wanted to spend more time writing. CNN insiders were hardly surprised, as Isaacson's unhappiness with the job was one of TV's worst-kept secrets.

"I love the ability to tell stories on TV," Isaacson says, but "I found at times TV personalities had a certain style to them where . . . you were managing a lot of egos—whether Aaron Brown and Lou Dobbs or Greta [were] worrying about their chairs, their cameras, who got what studio, who got to anchor the president, who got their show preempted when something [else] came on."

Isaacson denied that he was pushed from the company, yet his departure came amid a wave of defections from Turner Broadcasting and AOL Time Warner. Ted Turner left his largely ceremonial post as vice chairman of AOLTW, and Jamie Kellner announced he would step down as chief of Turner Broadcasting after just two years on the job. The exits were widely interpreted as proof that the merger of AOL and Time Warner was not working and that the combined company was strategically adrift.

Kellner concedes that his attempts to make CNN and Headline News more viewer-friendly had run into problems with the hard-core breaking-news types "who didn't want to see CNN change." Indeed, many in the Atlanta old guard seemed to take a cue from Ted Turner himself, contemptuously viewing Kellner and his team as Hollywood carpetbaggers. "If you talk about graphics and set design and things like that, [they] kind of looked down their nose a bit at you," Kellner says. "I doubt that they particularly enjoyed my tenure there."

Kellner was replaced by Phil Kent, the former president of the CNN News Group who had quit the company in 2001 when Isaacson came aboard. Kent's return was not generally well received. A handsome, blow-dried former CAA agent, Kent is widely regarded as a "suit"—a perfectly competent executive with no particular vision or urgency. "He's an old-time CNNer with no new game plan," media analyst and Turner biographer Porter Bibb told the Associated Press. "The problem CNN has is it is right now in free fall. They really need a dynamic leadership change."

To some, Isaacson's replacement was even more disappointing. Jim Walton had started at CNN twenty years earlier as a low-paid "veejay" and had spent most of his subsequent career in executive posts at CNN Sports. He is politically adept and well liked, but his hard news credentials are skimpy at best. Longtime Turner executive Robert Wussler calls

Walton a "nice guy" but "in the annals of journalism, not qualified to be the chairman of CNN." In a company beset by management turnover and internecine war, Walton was simply the "last Mohican standing," Wussler says.

Walton believed that CNN must return to its roots. "We have to understand who we are," he later told *The New York Times.* "And that is the Cable *News* Network." Like many in the Turner old guard, he was suspicious of Isaacson and Kellner's efforts to make the news more entertaining. He announced that he hated the informational "crawl" that was introduced after the September 11 terrorist attacks. Walton relented only after research indicated that 70 percent of viewers liked the feature. He also discontinued the two-hour weekly programming meetings attended by all senior managers, which had been instituted on Kellner's watch. Kellner had been schooled in these types of freewheeling meetings by his onetime mentor at Fox Broadcasting, Barry Diller, who felt that Socratic give-and-take was the best way to yield strong programming concepts. "The [new] people in charge don't want to be second-guessed, even in a small room with no one else around," one TBS executive says.

Walton thus did not make the most sympathetic audience for the likes of Connie Chung. CNN veterans already complained that her show's tabloid-style stories were junking up the network. So when she visited Walton to plead for the return of *Tonight,* the new CNN chairman took the opportunity to inform Chung that her show would not be returning—ever. He added that the network would find some other role for her. Chung was angry; her contract clearly promised her a prime-time slot, not some throwaway role. She told Walton she was quitting the network immediately.

For weeks Chung's agent negotiated the terms of her departure from CNN. In the end, the network agreed to keep paying her $2 million salary for the duration of her contract. CNN went for months without a permanent replacement program in the 8 P.M. slot opposite *The O'Reilly Factor.*

John Moody could not believe his eyes. Geraldo Rivera was on live television, drawing lines in the sand. The Fox News correspondent, accompanying soldiers from the 101st Airborne Division deep inside Iraq, was creating a makeshift map to tell viewers roughly where he was and in which direction the unit was heading. Moody, watching this in New York, realized it was a clear violation of Pentagon rules. As he saw Rivera work on his diagram, he says, "I shuddered."

As any American with a television knows, Rivera has a long history of controversy. He is an unabashed showboat, a latter-day P. T. Barnum with one foot in broadcasting and the other in vaudeville. In 1986 he hosted a one-hour special, *The Mystery of Al Capone's Vault,* which promised to unlock secrets of the legendary Chicago crime boss. Rivera found nothing inside the vault except dirt, but the program was the highest-rated syndicated special in TV history. The following year Rivera was hired by the Tribune Company to host *Geraldo,* a syndicated daytime talk show. The program quickly sank to previously unimaginable depths in a successful attempt to grab ratings. Rivera proudly noted that he single-handedly changed the direction of daytime TV with a program on "Men in Lace Panties and the Women Who Love Them." During a 1988 taping for *Geraldo,* a brawl broke out on the set between skinheads and the civil rights activist Roy Innis. Magazines nationwide carried photos of a bloodied and bandaged Rivera, whose nose was broken in the melee.

Less publicized were Rivera's battles with network executives. In 1985, while working for the ABC newsmagazine *20/20,* he attacked the network for killing a story on an alleged affair between President

Kennedy and Marilyn Monroe. Although Rivera had little to do with the segment, he took the principled stand that the network had violated journalistic freedom and engaged in a cover-up. "If a politician did this, we'd all do an exposé," Rivera told a reporter.

ABC News boss Roone Arledge, who had tolerated Rivera for years only because of his knack for ratings, quickly found an opportunity to rid himself of the mustached correspondent. "Geraldo's assistant/girlfriend—take your pick—was nabbed using an ABC messenger to pick up an ounce of marijuana," Arledge later wrote. Although Rivera denied involvement with the drug errand, he was ordered to resign, whereupon he embarked for the lucrative land of syndication.

After *Geraldo* ended its run, Rivera attempted to return to respectability with a prime-time show on CNBC, where he was hired by Roger Ailes. Many NBC News staffers were outraged. Brian Williams complained to Andy Lack, then the chief of NBC News. Lack explained that Rivera was a "big draw" on cable TV. "It's better to have him than compete against him," he told Williams. Nevertheless, friction with Tom Brokaw and others at NBC News persisted throughout Rivera's tenure at CNBC. In a 1998 interview with *TV Guide,* Rivera complained that Brokaw had banned promotions for *Geraldo Live* on the *NBC Nightly News.* He also suggested that he was "in the running" to replace Brokaw at the anchor desk, which did little to foster better relations with Brian Williams. Even Rivera's "apology" was self-serving: He told reporters that Brokaw was a great newsman, adding that "the rivalry between us is grossly overstated"—a backhanded way of letting readers know that Rivera fully considered himself Brokaw's rival.

Fox News hired Rivera in November 2001 as a war correspondent in Afghanistan. When the focus of the Bush administration shifted to Baghdad, Rivera was left hungering for the limelight. "He was itching to find a role in Iraq," Moody says. One day "he called, very excited, and said, 'Look, I can get airlifted from here directly to Kuwait.'" His bosses back in New York agreed, even though Rivera had not undergone the training embedded reporters were required to receive.

After the map incident, the Pentagon announced that it would immediately expel Rivera from Iraq. The public reaction from Fox News was muted. "It wasn't like the arrows that he drew in the sand were secret information," Moody says. "*The Washington Post,* literally two days earlier, had a very similar map. . . . But technically, it was a violation of the embedment rules." Rivera said that he knew nothing about an expulsion order and blamed "some rats" from NBC, his former employer, for spreading rumors about him.

In fact, Rivera had worked out a deal with the Pentagon: He agreed to undergo formal embedment training in Kuwait and then petition to get back into Iraq. Many at Fox News decided that Rivera had turned into a huge embarrassment and had to go. He was also expensive; news staffers pointed out that three or four top-notch reporters could be hired for Rivera's $2 million salary. But when staffers insisted that the wayward correspondent be fired, Ailes flatly refused. Rivera was a loyal network employee, and to the Fox News chairman it seemed unfair to ax him because of the map-drawing imbroglio.

As it happened, Fox News need not have worried. Other networks were suffering their own wartime embarrassments. MSNBC, for instance, featured some Baghdad dispatches from Peter Arnett, CNN's onetime star, who like Rivera seemed unable to stay out of trouble. Not long after Gulf War II started, Arnett gave an interview to state-run Iraqi TV in which he said that the Pentagon's initial war plan had failed because of stiff resistance from Hussein's forces. Although NBC initially defended Arnett, he was soon sacked by NBC News president Neil Shapiro.

Viewers generally seemed to accept the map affair as yet another instance of Geraldo being Geraldo. Fox News suffered little long-term damage from the incident outside of some one-liners from late-night comics. As NBC's Conan O'Brien joked, "If Geraldo is kicked out, this means that Saddam Hussein will once again be the most hated man in Iraq."

Baghdad fell on April 11. That morning, with Saddam Hussein's regime crumbling, *The New York Times* published a remarkable op-ed by Eason Jordan.

Headlined THE NEWS WE KEPT TO OURSELVES, the article described how over the past twelve years CNN had withheld numerous stories of atrocities in Iraq, "awful things that could not be reported because doing so would have jeopardized the lives of Iraqis, particularly those on our Baghdad staff."

Jordan revealed that in the mid-1990s an Iraqi cameraman working for CNN was given electroshock torture by Saddam Hussein's secret police because he would not confirm that Jordan was a CIA operative. One government aide had his front teeth ripped out with pliers for displeasing Saddam's son Uday; he was told never to wear dentures "so he would always remember the price to be paid for upsetting his boss." Uday himself had boasted to Jordan that he would kill two of his brothers-in-law who had fled the country; the men were later lured back to Iraq and murdered.

"I felt awful having these stories bottled up inside me," Jordan wrote. "At last, these stories can be told freely."

Later that day Jordan told National Public Radio, "There's been a bit of a fuss about the op-ed piece." That was putting it mildly. Many at CNN felt blindsided—not so much by Jordan's revelations about life in Iraq but that he had gone public with an admission that the network had purposely withheld legitimate news stories. Jordan had only casually mentioned to other executives the idea of writing the piece, one insider says, and had never discussed it with the PR department at CNN. Reporters who called the network for elaboration were told that Jordan committed a faux pas out of sheer exhaustion; he was working virtually nonstop covering the war, pausing only to catch catnaps at the Omni Hotel inside CNN Center.

The reaction outside the network was considerably less accommodating. Rival journalists accused CNN of trading its integrity for access—and, indeed, Jordan's earlier comments about "trying to own the story" in Iraq underscored the network's eagerness to keep a presence in the country. Some of the harshest reaction came, predictably, from Murdoch's *New York Post,* which compared CNN's actions in Iraq to those of Nazi appeasers during World War II. "If you can't report the truth," Eric Fettmann wrote in a *Post* opinion piece, "why have journalists [in Baghdad] in the first place? . . . CNN's silence seems to have cost as many lives as it saved."

The Jordan article was not nearly as damaging to CNN as the Tailwind scandal; some journalists even leaped to the network's defense, arguing that reporting on a dangerous regime inevitably involves painful trade-offs and that Jordan made the correct choice in putting the safety of his staff first. But the incident heightened a sense of frustration within CNN. Not only was Fox News trouncing CNN in the ratings, but it also appeared to be held to a different journalistic standard. Silly Geraldo Rivera blithely violated Pentagon rules and became a late-night joke; serious Eason Jordan unloaded his conscience of sins of omission and became a besieged journalistic case study.

"I was surprised to some degree by some of the responses to the article," Jordan says. "But I stand by everything that was in it. If I could do it all over again, I would do it a little bit differently, in stressing that CNN had reported many, many times—with its own reporting and by putting guests on the air—on the brutality of the [Iraqi] regime. There was no doubt about that."

Despite Eason Jordan's vow, CNN did not dominate coverage of Gulf War II.

During the first week of the war, Fox News averaged 5.6 million prime-time viewers, compared to 4.4 million for CNN and 2.2 million for MSNBC. Fox had over the previous year developed a stranglehold on the ratings race, and even another round of war in the Persian Gulf could not help CNN break it. As every TV executive learns, once viewing habits develop, they are very hard to break.

But Fox did come in for some aggressive criticism of its flag-waving war coverage, which made even some network insiders privately uncomfortable. Neil Cavuto, anchor of *Your World,* dismissed war protesters as "sickening." John Gibson complained of "the dopey old U.N." *The New York Times* referred to a "Fox effect" on television news, noting that third-place MSNBC had gone as far as hiring right-wing radio host Michael Savage, who accused war protesters of committing sedition and treason. (Savage was dismissed weeks later for making anti-gay remarks.)

The *Times* crowned Fox "the most-watched source of cable news by far, with anchors and commentators who skewer the mainstream media, disparage the French and flay anybody else who questions President Bush's war effort."

To many at Fox News, that is how it should be. The network insisted it was winning *because* of—not in spite of—its jingoistic approach. When reminded of critics who attacked Fox for referring to U.S. soldiers as "our troops," anchor Shepard Smith replies with a spirited rejoinder that could almost serve as the Fox News creed.

"Fuck them," Smith says to the critics. "They *are* our troops. . . . Waving the flag? [Terrorists] knocked the fucking buildings down, down the street on 9/11. That's where the flag [on Fox's screen] started.

We needed a little something to rally around. I admit no apologies. I think the vast majority of Americans are absolutely on board with that. They understand that we can be credible journalists, fair and balanced about everything that we do, and still be for our side.

"Once we're in this war, it's us against them," Smith says. "And we're going to win."

Epilogue

On a balmy evening in June 2003, the stars of Fox News crammed into a new street-level studio, just around the corner from the entrance to the News Corporation building in midtown Manhattan.

Bill O'Reilly was there, his lanky frame rising above the crowd. Greta Van Susteren showed up, as did Sean Hannity and Alan Colmes and Neil Cavuto. Geraldo Rivera and his soon-to-be fifth wife, Erica Levy, chatted and joked with Roger Ailes.

The occasion was the unveiling of Studio D, the new home of *DaySide with Linda Vester,* Fox's daytime talk show. After allowing the guests to mingle for a half hour or so, Ailes ascended to the platform stage and raised his arms to hush everyone.

His bald crown rimmed with white hair, Ailes proudly noted that Fox News held a two-to-one ratings advantage over CNN, a seemingly unthinkable prospect just two years earlier. Even CNN's once invincible *Larry King Live* was losing its luster. The only time the program had beaten Fox recently was when Bob Hope died and King aired an old interview with the comic, filmed "back when he was ninety-seven," Ailes joked.

The Vester studio replaced a Chinese restaurant that had gone out of business. Ailes said that the eatery had gone downhill "ever since they ran out of sweet-and-sour cat." The crowd tittered.

"One thing about me, I'm often not politically correct," Ailes continued. "I can say what I want and they can't get me, because I'll sue them for age discrimination."

Still, it was a fairly subdued performance, at least by Ailesian standards. But then, Ailes had been keeping a low profile in recent months, even as Fox News solidified its position as the undisputed leader in cable news. He was bruised after reporter Bob Woodward, in his best-seller *Bush at War,* revealed that the Fox News chairman had sent President Bush a private memo containing political advice after the terrorist attacks of September 11. Editorialists chided Ailes for violating journalistic objectivity. Insiders speculated that the source of the story was White House adviser Karl Rove, who is said to resent Ailes's ties to the Bush family.

Asked whether he thought Rove was involved, Ailes replies, "I don't have any idea." But possibly to avoid such embarrassments in the future, Ailes claims he's virtually sworn off talking to journalists—an odd position for the chief of a news network.

"I've gone almost totally underground," he says. "I'm just not talking to anybody anymore, ever again, as long as I live."

There might have been another reason for his reticence. Ailes was nearing the end of his Fox News contract and was said to desire a larger role within News Corporation. It remained unclear whether Rupert Murdoch was inclined to give him one.

Ailes does little to dispel the notion that he might leave Fox News soon. He says it's "unclear in my own mind" how long he'll stay, adding: "I'm here for a while."

The inevitability of the boss's exit is a taboo subject at Fox News, akin to broaching the idea of papal fallibility in St. Peter's Square.

"As far as I'm concerned, he's not leaving," says Fox producer Bill Shine. "It's natural to think about, but no one thinks about it."

At CNN, staffers were still getting accustomed to the most recent management shakeup.

New president Jim Walton sought to reassure veterans that there was little chance the network would move from CNN Center, despite persistent rumors to the contrary. "CNN will always be based in Atlanta," he told TV critics in early June.

The once-dominant network seemed to have settled into a distant second place behind Fox, with no clear path toward retaking the ratings crown. Walton tried to steer a middle course between Turner's "news is the star" mantra and Fox's personality-centered approach.

"I think people watch *people,*" Walton told *The New York Times* later that summer. "I do believe it matters who viewers allow into their homes. It's not just the news."

CNN continued to downplay the Fox competition publicly, but at CNN Center, staffers could not forget the rivalry even if they wanted to.

Shortly after Eason Jordan wrote his notorious *New York Times* op-ed piece about withholding stories in Saddam Hussein's Iraq, Fox News outbid CNN for a huge billboard across the street from CNN Center, at an estimated cost of $25,000 per month. AMERICA TRUSTS FOX NEWS, the sign read, along with the text: *We believe the press should not be a lap dog for dictators or an attack dog against our country, but a watchdog for everyone.*

The message may have made tourists scratch their heads, but it was clearly visible from the second-story restaurant at the Omni Hotel where many CNN executives took their lunch.

Meanwhile, MSNBC fell into an even deeper funk as its ratings continued to decline.

For May 2003, the network lost nearly 7 percent of its total primetime audience compared to the same period a year earlier (CNN was flat and Fox News soared 58 percent). Over the total day, Fox was averaging nearly four times as many viewers as MSNBC.

Keith Olbermann, the quirky host of *The Big Show* during the early promising years of MSNBC, returned to the network with a new prime-time program, although it failed to generate much enthusiasm among viewers.

Some staffers despaired of the network ever finding the right formula; the success of Fox News led others to certain fatalism about TV journalism itself.

Brian Williams, the former MSNBC anchor who will take over Tom Brokaw's anchor desk after the 2004 elections, sounds a general note of pessimism about the fate of the business. "I'm pretty convinced I'll be the last guy doing the news in a tie," he says. Williams became close to former CBS News president Dick Salant shortly before he died. "I think about him every day, and I am probably glad that he . . . didn't see what happened to his beloved television news business. Christ, look at what's happened. Grab any newscast off the shelf from ten years ago. We are a totally different business. And I am not being melodramatic when I say that when I take over for Tom, I really do have an obligation and a responsibility to the viewers, to the folks at NBC News, to keep entertainment from further encroaching on the straight and narrow."

He adds: "Think of what now makes it as a story. [Murder victim] Laci Peterson, police chases, all this stuff that gets its own music and animation and titles and specials. Oh, my God."

Ailes spoke only a few minutes in Studio D, and after he finished, there was little to do besides listen to a live band and eat hors d'oeuvres. Guests slowly drifted off, clutching gift bags of martini shakers with matching glasses.

Some of them walked the half-block east to Sixth Avenue to hail a cab. At the corner, if they stopped for a moment and looked one block south, the Fox guests could see a giant billboard at Forty-seventh Street. The ad appeared to be aimed directly at the second-story windows of Fox executives a stone's throw away. Dominated by the image of a smiling Aaron Brown, the sign urged passersby to watch CNN.

NOTES

In the text, direct quotations that are tagged using the present tense ("he says") indicate material culled from author interviews. The past tense ("he said") indicates a quotation obtained from a secondary source.

Prologue

1 *"You're worse than the American administration":* "Nic Robertson: 'We didn't want to push our luck,'" an interview posted on CNN.com, March 22, 2003.

Chapter 1: "One Giant Leap"

5 *"Surprise!" the president of NBC joked:* Details of the press conference announcing MSNBC were obtained from an NBC videotape of the event, along with author interviews with participants and contemporary press accounts.

6 *Wright traveled so much:* Ken Auletta, *Three Blind Mice: How the TV Networks Lost Their Way* (New York: Random House, 1991).

12 *"we were going to have egg on our face":* Peter Neupert, author interview, May 23, 2003.

14 *"Jack, do you believe the cable forecasts?":* This and the exchange immediately following are drawn from Jack Welch (with John A. Byrne), *Jack: Straight from the Gut* (New York: Warner Business Books, 2001).

16 *"He was interested, but it wasn't possible":* Bob Wright, author interview, February 11, 2003.

Chapter 2: Television Is Not a Gimmick

21 *One month . . . dozens of CNBC employees:* Details of this meeting were obtained from a CNBC videotape of the event as well as author interviews.

22 *"I knew they might pull a fast one":* Roger Ailes, author interview, November 12, 2002.

23 *"Murdoch seems to be most interested":* James Fallows, "The Age of Murdoch," *The Atlantic Monthly,* September 2003.

23 *"Fortune favors the brave":* Quoted by Warner Bros. Television president Peter Roth in luncheon remarks at the Museum of Television & Radio in Beverly Hills, October 14, 2003.

25 *"He had the drive, the energy":* Chet Collier, author interview, August 5, 2003.

26 *"didn't want to do much of anything":* Roger Ailes, author interview, August 4, 2003.

27 *"On the show, he was more enthusiastic":* Mike Douglas (with Thomas Kelly and Michael Heaton), *I'll Be Right Back: Memories of TV's Greatest Talk Show* (New York: Simon & Schuster, 2000).

27 *"I'm going to fire this fucking director":* Joe McGinnis, *The Selling of the President* (New York: Trident Press, 1969).

28 *"the kind of kid who always carried a bookbag":* McGinnis, *The Selling of the President.*

30 *"Don't ever chase critics":* Ailes interview, August 4, 2003.

31 *"Tell your goddamned network":* Laurence Zuckerman and Richard Stengel, "Bushwacked! Dan Rather Sets Sparks Flying in a Showdown with the Vice President," *Time,* February 8, 1988.

Chapter 3: This . . . Is CNN

40 *"We call it the Biosphere":* Bill Hemmer, author interview, July 10, 2003.

41 *"he walked in the newsroom at four in the morning":* Eason Jordan, author interview, July 25, 2003.

41 *"The old wives' tale":* Robert Wussler, author interview, July 16, 2003.

42 *"Oh, a million a year":* Reese Schonfeld, *Me and Ted Against the World: The Unauthorized Story of the Founding of CNN* (New York: Cliff Street, 2001).

44 *"I loved Ed":* Steve Haworth, author interview, July 18, 2003.

45 *"I thought [Amos] would take":* Lou Dobbs, author interview, June 18, 2003.

47 *"Would you really accept":* Tom Johnson, author interview (via email), May 7, 2003.

50 *"You guys just keep covering the news":* Haworth interview, July 18, 2003.

52 *"Ted had a habit":* Reese Schonfeld, author interview, July 3, 2003.

54 *Johnson sent the senior production team a memo:* Anita Sharpe, "CNN Sticks with Hard News as Ratings Fall," *The Wall Street Journal,* June 9, 1994.

Chapter 4: Squish Rupert Like a Bug

57 *"Get the deal done":* James Bates and Claudia Eller, "Creating an Entertainment Giant," *Los Angeles Times,* September 23, 1995.

59 *"We went to everybody":* Robert Wussler, author interview, July 16, 2003.

60 *"There was a lot of heat":* Tom Rogers, author interview, May 28, 2003.

61 *Ted Turner and Bill Gates were watching TV:* Peter Neupert, author interview, May 23, 2003.

63 *Malone was insisting on a number of provisions:* Steve McClellan, "It's TBS Time," *Broadcasting & Cable,* September 25, 1995.

65 *"For a whole generation of us":* Andy Lack, author interview, November 26, 2002.

Chapter 5: An Imaginary Friend

73 *"I did win one nice battle":* John Moody, author interview, April 23, 2003.

73 *"One of the problems we have to work on":* Moody interview, April 23, 2003.

75 *Financial analysts . . . up to $400 million:* Roone Arledge, *Roone: A Memoir* (New York: HarperCollins, 2003).

76 *"As the new competition emerged":* Tom Johnson, author interview (via email), July 9, 2003.

76 *Each was offered $7 million:* Johnson interview, July 9, 2003.

79 *"We were trying to get people from the White House":* Bill Shine, author interview, June 19, 2003.

79 *Moody traveled to Washington:* Moody interview, April 23, 2003.

Chapter 6: Fair and Balanced

86 *"If you talk to journalists":* Brit Hume, author interview, August 5, 2003.

87 *"Every night Cronkite signed off:* Richard Salant, "Letter to the Editor," *The Wall Street Journal,* April 5, 1985. Salant was responding to a March 28, 1985, *Journal* editorial that said Walter Cronkite had "editorialized" during his years on the *CBS Evening News.*

87 *"Those things might have happened":* Peter J. Boyer, *Who Killed CBS?: The Undoing of America's Number One News Network* (New York: Random House, 1988).

Chapter 7: Is Ted Turner Nuts?

94 *"What the hell happened?":* Bryan Burrough and Kim Masters, "Cable Guys," *Vanity Fair,* January 1997.

96 *"I learned firsthand how the sytem works":* Lawrence K. Grossman, "Bullies on the Block," *Columbia Journalism Review,* January/February 1997.

98 *When Dressler informed NBC:* Burrough and Masters, "Cable Guys."

99 *"You don't have to be a rocket scientist":* Ted Turner deposition, October 18, 1996, *Time Warner Cable v. The City of New York and Bloomberg LP,* in U.S. District Court, Southern District of New York.

99 *"You're not taking the long-term view":* Burrough and Masters, "Cable Guys."

99 *Turner called Time Warner Cable:* Turner deposition, October 18, 1996.

100 *"By the time of the party, it was pretty clear":* Clifford J. Levy, "Lobbying at Murdoch Gala Ignited New York Cable Clash," *The New York Times,* October 13, 1996.

Chapter 8: "Valley of Death"

108 *"I just got off the phone with Henry Kissinger":* April Oliver, author interview, July 7, 2003. Oliver was not present in Atlanta but participated in the meeting by teleconference. Tom Johnson confirmed that he spoke with Kissinger and other former high-ranking government officials about the Tailwind story prior to assigning Floyd Abrams and David Kohler to review the report.

109 *The night the report aired:* Mary Murphy and Dennis McDougal, "Tailwind: Behind the TV Story of the Year," *TV Guide,* December 26, 1998. This was the first part of a four-part Tailwind investigation.

110 *"He knew a good story":* Jeff Gralnick, author interview, August 1, 2003.

110 *"I wish you would die of cancer":* The source for this quotation witnessed the incident firsthand but declined to be identified.

112 *"Make Kaplan president":* Schonfeld, *Me and Ted Against the World.*

113 *"Rick's [domestic channel] was given the highest priority":* Tom Johnson, author interview (via email), July 14, 2003.

114 *"I'm nervous about this story":* The source is a firsthand witness who declined to be identified.

114 *Rick Kaplan was also confident:* Murphy and McDougal, "Tailwind: Behind the TV Story of the Year."

120 *"Tom Johnson . . . absolutely panicked":* Oliver interview, July 7, 2003.

120 *"It felt like . . . giant group therapy":* Greta Van Susteren, author interview, April 11, 2003.

121 *"Rick is in my opinion":* Lou Dobbs, author interview, June 18, 2003.

Chapter 9: Fake Brick and Aunt Fanny

126 *"What are you doing?":* Phil Griffin, author interview, September 18, 2003.

127 *"GE . . . was pressing NBC":* Andy Lack, author interview, November 26, 2002.

128 *"I point to the areas":* Leonard Downie Jr. and Robert G. Kaiser, *The News About the News: American Journalism in Peril* (New York: Vintage Books, 2002).

129 *Lack "gave NBC News":* Brian Williams, author interview, July 15, 2003.

130 *"Do you need me":* Griffin interview, September 18, 2003.

134 *"We felt that the structure":* Peter Neupert, author interview, May 23, 2003.

Chapter 10: The Right Person

139 *"Bill just wasn't taking":* Bill Shine, author interview, June 19, 2003.

140 *Later, in his best-seller:* Bill O'Reilly, *The No-Spin Zone: Confrontations with the Powerful and Famous in America* (New York: Broadway Books, 2001).

140 *"If I have any ability":* Roger Ailes, author interview, November 12, 2002.

141 *"I think I listened":* Chet Collier, author interview, August 5, 2003.

143 *"I'm not sure where the business is going":* Neil Swidey, "The Meanest Man on Television," *Boston Globe Magazine,* December 1, 2002; also Glenn Garvin, "Bill O'Reilly, the Equal Opportunity Terrorizer," *The Miami Herald,* July 7, 2003.

144 *"The show was a little softer":* Bill O'Reilly, author interview, December 15, 2002.

Chapter 11: Electoral Follies

147 *Shortly before midnight:* John Moody, author interview, April 28, 2003.

150 *"I'll never forget the morning":* David Brock, "Roger Ailes Is Mad As Hell," *New York,* November 17, 1997.

150 *"On an average news day":* Marshall Sella, "The Red State Network," *The New York Times Magazine,* June 24, 2001.

151 *Fox News "got an enormous lift":* Bob Wright, author interview, February 11, 2003.

152 *"I think Rick":* Steve Haworth, author interview, July 18, 2003.

153 *"Many criticized me":* Tom Johnson, author interview (via email), July 14, 2003.

157 *"My thought . . . was that Republicans":* Brit Hume, author interview, August 5, 2003.

Chapter 12: Waving the Flag

161 *He was in the middle of the 8:30 meeting:* John Moody, author interview, May 7, 2003.

163 *She was spending the morning at home:* Paula Zahn, author interview, July 10, 2003.

165 *"Pittman . . . said he felt":* Jamie Kellner, author interview, April 17, 2003.

165 *"We started doing talent meetings":* Garth Ancier, author interview, April 21, 2003.

167 *"You look at stuff that's gone through":* Moody interview, April 23, 2003.

168 *"Well, Walter, even the Seven Years' War":* Walter Isaacson, interview, April 28, 2003.

168 *"It was not a great job":* Isaacson interview, April 28, 2003.

Chapter 13: A Dead Raccoon

173 *Her set for* The Point*:* Greta Van Susteren, author interview, April 11, 2003.

175 *"Perusing its one-hundred-plus pages":* Arledge, *Roone: A Memoir.*

183 *"I thought it was despicable":* Van Susteren interview, April 11, 2003.

184 *"Which is why":* Walter Isaacson, author interview, April 28, 2003.

184 *"Greta was looking":* Jamie Kellner, author interview, April 17, 2003.

Chapter 14: War and Ratings

189 *"It was one of the few times in my career":* John Moody, author interview, June 18, 2003.

192 *"I started feeling like the attractive Munster daughter":* Brian Williams, author interview, July 15, 2003.

193 *"He made his name convincing all the women":* Roger Ailes, author interview, November 12, 2002.

193 *"I kind of thought Donahue":* Walter Isaacson, author interview, April 28, 2003.

198 *"I don't see twenty-four-hour news as a business":* Jamie Kellner, author interview, April 17, 2003.

Chapter 15: "A Line in the Sand"

200 *Eason Jordan held the phone:* Eason Jordan, author interview, July 25, 2003.

201 *"We certainly recognized that CNN was not dead":* John Moody, author interview, June 18, 2003.

204 *"I love the ability to tell stories on TV":* Walter Issacson, author interview, April 28, 2003.

205 *"If you talk about graphics and set design":* Jamie Kellner, author interview, April 17, 2003.

206 *"last Mohican standing":* Robert Wussler, author interview, July 16, 2003.

208 *"It's better to have him":* Brian Williams, author interview, July 15, 2003.

211 *"I was surprised":* Jordan interview, July 25, 2003.

212 *"Fuck them":* Shepard Smith, author interview, June 19, 2003.

Epilogue

214 *On a balmy evening in June 2003:* The author attended the event described.

215 *"I've gone almost totally underground":* Roger Ailes, author interview, August 4, 2003.

217 *"I'm pretty convinced I'll be the last guy":* Brian Williams, author interview, July 15, 2003.

INDEX